# SAMMY DAVIS JR.

## *The Writer Who Saved His Estate*

Pamela A. Sherrod

ISBN 9780692587867

ISBN 10: 0692587861
RisingStar31 Productions
P.O. Box 20071
Bradenton, Florida 34204
www.risingstar31.com

Printed in the United States of America

# TABLE OF CONTENTS

# INTRODUCTION

When Altovise Davis suddenly died and my fiancé committed suicide thirty-five days later, I felt like the last little Indian in the morbid poem I'd read as a child. For me, it marked the culmination of several years of bizarre events that had not only shocked me, but essentially changed my life. During that particular year, in the spring of 2009, I was paralyzed by, both, inescapable sorrow and a deep sense of guilt. "Had I pushed them too far?" I wondered, fearing that I'd given them a false sense of hope.

The sad irony was that, I'd saved the Sammy Davis Jr. estate, but failed to save Altovise, who'd inherited it. She was not only my writing partner, but a close friend, and I felt like I'd let her down. So, I shut down the production plans for a musical film we'd written, abandoning the most compelling work I'd ever started.

When I looked back, I mused over the fact that I'd unwittingly stumbled into one of Hollywood's most vicious battles, a fight over who would control the legal rights to Sammy Davis Jr.'s image, copyrights and royalty payments. It was the lawsuit that blocked the production of a major motion picture about his life, and, if there was any entertainer whose life had warranted a film, it was Sammy Davis Jr.

The Rat Pack star had never failed to trigger the intensive scrutiny from the media, and this applied to the explosive episodes of his fabled life and the disturbing events which followed his death. In many ways, he shared this trait with his wife.

Altovise Davis experienced, both, the blessings and curses of being married to an international sensation. Sammy Davis Jr. was the phenomenal African American star who'd torn down many of the entertainment industry's racial boundaries to become a larger-than-life legend. Known as 'The World's Greatest Entertainer,' Sammy was multi-talented and driven by something far beyond most people's reach. From his tap-dancing debut as a three-year-old vaudeville 'midget,' to the televised star-studded tribute to his career, six decades later, he sang, danced, rendered impersonations, and delivered stunning acting performances that inspired artists like Michael Jackson and dazzled fans from around the world. For Sammy, showbusiness had been, not only his home, but his one true love.

Admittedly, when I was growing up, I didn't know much about Sammy Davis – nor, the other Rat Pack members, for that matter – but, I was aware that my parents were strangely quiet about the entertainer, apparently having reservations about his swinging lifestyle and swaying political loyalties. I'd heard some grumblings from friends and relatives about Sammy having hugged President Nixon in public, which, in many black communities was simply deplorable. Ingratiating himself with a Republican, in their eyes, had made him the quintessential traitor.

Personally, I really didn't think much about it. After all, I was just a laidback kid, and as my father said, "A real New England Yankee."

My limited perceptions of Sammy were formed by what I'd seen on television, especially during the early 1970's. He appeared to be a somewhat comical character who was always on the tube: one night on **Rowan and Martin's Laugh-In;** on another occasion, **The Hollywood Squares.**

Of course, in later years, I'd hear the news reports about Sammy's death, the insolvency of his estate, and the $5 million debt he'd left his widow. However, the reports wouldn't begin to address the depth and complexity of his legacy.

Sammy's international fame was earned, not solely from his extraordinary talent, but his tumultuous life, the backdrop of which was initially dramatized – or, in Sammy's case, traumatized – by economic hardships during The Depression and, then, brutal encounters with racism, particularly in the United States Army.

Beginning in the late 1920's, when racial intolerance was near a peak, Sammy traveled through the Vaudeville circuit with his father, Samuel Davis, Sr., an entertainer, and Will Mastin, whom he called 'uncle.' Segregation laws was enforced in much of the country, although Sammy wasn't quite aware of it, at the time. His father had consistently devised creative ways to shield him from this.

Sammy's mother, Elvera Sanchez, was an Afro-Cuban entertainer who was, for the most part, absent from his life. Sammy initially said she was Puerto-Rican, due to the era's anti-Cuban Cold War sentiment. Elvera, however, was first, and foremost, a showgirl. She divorced her husband when Sammy was three years old, opting to independently forge her own career. Single-minded, ambitious and emotionally detached, the quiet joys of parenthood couldn't compete with the applause of an audience. Oddly enough, Elvera would impart this trait to her son, as it was replicated in his relationship with his own children.

Sammy's entrance into show business happened rather spontaneously, because it wasn't actually planned. One day, after watching numerous stage acts and individual performances, the courageous three-year-old simply strutted across the stage, where he began lifting and shuffling his feet, in an effort to imitate the dance moves he'd seen his father and Will Mastin make. For an awkward moment, there was a silent pause. When the audience roared with laughter, Will Mastin, who'd formed and managed his troupe, noticed a magical connection that the boy had made. Being a wise businessman, he immediately spotted the ultimate answer – a powerful weapon they could use to sustain them in a dying industry – a gifted child.

Little Sammy became, not only a 'working man,' but the group's main source of bread and butter. The magical element of a child performer helped Will Mastin's trio scrape through some of the worst years of The Great Depression. The cinema grew; less fortunate groups were forced to fold up and shut down. Although, Sammy's performances were the saving grace for the group, it came at a high cost and personal sacrifice for the young boy, who didn't realize at the time the significance of what he'd traded.

Sammy never attended school, and missed getting the formal education needed to read and write. Sam Sr. and Will would vigilantly look out for truancy officers, and whenever one was spotted, they'd send Sammy Jr. scampering into a closet, or another convenient hiding spot. Not only was truancy from school an issue to contend with, but the country's child labor laws.

Altovise once told me that, to avoid detection of Sammy's true age, his father and uncle initially passed him off as a midget. For a while, like many other child performers, Sammy was enrolled in a correspondence course, but it failed to provide him with a sound educational background.

Child's play was also foreign to young Sammy. He often watched with curiosity, as other children his age laughed and skipped on playgrounds and competitively engaged in sports. Their trio couldn't afford to take a chance on Sammy suffering an injury – not even a small one. So, no sports were permitted. Instead, Sam Sr. and Will lavished him with ice cream treats and comic books, the pages of which were always filled with more pictures than words.

What Sammy did study and practice avidly were the professional routines of the show people around him – their stage songs, dance moves and comical skits. Like a sponge, he soaked up everything he saw, practicing the moves over and over, until he perfected and improved on them. With his small, lithe body, he poured his boundless energy and passion into his work, and the results began to pay off. Sammy became limitless in executing every move with grace, style and speed.

Before long, the young boy showed a special talent, when it came to hoofing with the trio, and he began to delight audiences around the country. By the age of four, Sammy had performed in several cities, and when he was seven, appeared in his first feature film with the actress, Ethel Waters. It was called *Rufus Jones for President.*

Although, the movie depicted the most unflattering and demeaning stereotypes of blacks, the film offered viewers an unforgettable display of Sammy's remarkable dancing and singing skills. Completely confident before the cameras, he delivered an impassioned performance that dazzled the audience.

It was during World War II, when Sammy was eighteen years old, that he was drafted and assigned to one of the first integrated infantries in the U. S. Army. There, he faced the brunt of unbridled racial hatred, the type that some people went to great lengths to express. All of his life, Sammy had been shielded from discrimination by his father and uncle, and he was grossly unprepared to handle the intensity of the racism and segregationist sentiment of the early 1940's.

His enemies would give him a crash course on discrimination, enlisting their own savage methods in the process. There was one recruit, in particular, who slept in the bed next to Sammy's, and started trouble almost immediately after arriving. His name was Jennings, and he was relentless in his abuse of Davis. An assignment on the front lines, facing the actual enemy, couldn't have been a more brutal experience.

Sammy was especially proud of a watch he'd brought. He took exceptional care of the timepiece, because his father and Will had sacrificed $150 of their rent money to buy the gift. It was a gold chronograph, which was popular with Air Force pilots.

One day, when Sammy accidently dropped the watch, Jennings quickly seized the opportunity to step on it, cracking the glass, twisting the gold and mangling its hands. The timepiece was completely destroyed. Chuckling about it, he told Sammy that he could simply steal another one.

Unfortunately, Sammy's watch wouldn't be the only thing that was broken. Bullied and coerced into violent confrontations, Sammy's nose was bloodied and broken on three separate occasions. Since there were few, if any, protections for black soldiers, his tormenters plastered him with paint, tried to trick him into drinking a man's urine and then poured it down his pants.

The severity of their treatment, and Sammy's insatiable need to overcome it, would ultimately fuel his determination to be a great performer. When Sammy was transferred to Special Services – the entertainment division – his extraordinary talent earned for him a new level of respect. The cheers and applause effectively melted the wall of hatred and became Sammy's most powerful weapon in combating discrimination.

Sammy, who hadn't gone to school and couldn't read or write, was exposed to several books provided by one of his sergeants. Anxious to learn, Sammy would stay up late at night, just to study the pages of the written word. Still, when it came to performing on written tests, he was hindered by his lack of formal training. Davis became painfully aware of the limited nature of his prospects for the future: he was unattractive, uneducated and unaccepted. When he weighed all the options, it was obvious that, if he was ever going to be successful, he'd have to depend on his gifts as an entertainer.

When Sammy was discharged from the service, he continued performing with his father and Will Mastin. This time, though, he saw the world as it truly was. Sam Sr. could no longer disguise or filter the discrimination they'd always faced. None of the old sugar-coated excuses could be used; they lodged on the black side of town because it was the only place where they were welcomed. Black entertainers were treated differently from white performers and now he knew why.

Sammy had an insatiable desire to become a star, and there was nothing that could hold him down. Although, he'd suffered many daunting challenges, he was extremely driven and his talent would grow stronger each year. In fact, when Sammy suffered the loss of an eye after a life-threatening auto accident, his tenacity and courage would be demonstrated when he returned to the stage.

Only a few years earlier, Sammy's career had taken off.

In 1951, on the evening of the Academy Awards, Sammy, along with his father and Will Mastin, gave the explosive performance that catapulted him into stardom. At Ciro's Nightclub, the alluring entertainer, Janis Paige, was the headliner for the event, however, the patrons were given an unexpected treat. The three hoofers danced with everything they had, virtually, tearing up the floor and tearing down the place. The crowd jumped to their feet, slammed their forks on the table and loudly clamored for more.

When Sammy broke into his impersonations of several famous celebrities, the stunned audience, laughed uncontrollably. Noticing Jerry Lewis in the crowd, he took a big gamble, and launched into a Jerry Lewis imitation. When Lewis screamed with delight, the audience went completely wild.

That night, Sammy and the Mastin Trio turned the corner, and their lives would be changed forever.

Looking back, it's ironic that, on the evening of the Academy Awards, some fifty-six years later, another pivotal moment would occur – only it was much more subdued, in comparison – but, it would ultimately impact the legacy of Sammy's work and determine the outcome of his troubled estate.

Although Sammy went on to become a famous entertainer, it wouldn't diminish his admiration of other artists, many of whom he photographed with the zeal of a young star-struck fan. Sammy relished his access to some of the world's most iconic figures: Elvis Pressley and Marilyn Monroe; Michael Jackson and Lucille Ball; Humphrey Bogart and Bill Cosby. Secretly, he helped Elizabeth Taylor and Richard Burton begin the torrid love affair that led to their first marriage, and once, during an ugly dispute in Monaco, he defiantly refused to perform for Princess Grace.

Sammy, himself, would be immortalized in the photographs of him beside his long-time buddy, Frank Sinatra, and other legendary members of The Rat Pack. Sammy and Frank, in fact, would be much more than just friends.

Back in 1945, when Sammy was about 20 years old, he'd waited outside with hundreds of screaming (and often fainting) young fans to see his idol, Frank Sinatra, after one of his performances. Frank was called "The Voice," because one could literally turn on the radio and hear him crooning on multiple stations. Sammy took great pride in the fact that he (and the Will Mastin Trio) had opened for Sinatra, about five years earlier, before his career had taken off. Remarkably, Frank would also remember Sammy.

Frank was a very strong advocate of racial tolerance and made a point of using black entertainers to open his acts. He'd eventually take Sammy under his wing, using his considerable power to open doors that no one else could. Frank helped Sammy break into establishments where he was previously barred and opened opportunities that were unprecedented for black performers.

One night, after Sammy was denied entry into New York's Copacabana Club, Frank, who was performing there, reserved a table especially for him. Then, Sinatra, in his notoriously forceful manner, insisted that Sammy return to the segregated club, this time, alone. Davis was hesitant, but when he finally arrived, he was politely escorted to his table, where he was treated as Frank's special guest.

Frank would later tell Sammy, "Anything I can ever do for you – you've got yourself a friend for life."

Frank's declaration of loyalty turned out to be a lasting promise. The two men established a bond that survived the ups and downs of their careers – and a couple of fallouts – and represented one of the most prolific friendships in the entertainment industry.

Nowhere was this more evident than in Las Vegas, where the two entertainers would dominate the scene for many years. In fact, the Rat Pack stars literally ruled Las Vegas, and although the group was initially conceived by Humphrey Bogart and his wife, actress Lauren Bacall, it would almost always refer to the flamboyant group of friends that included Frank Sinatra, Sammy Davis Jr., Dean Martin, Joey Bishop and Peter Lawford (President John F. Kennedy's brother-in-law).

They were the cool cats who strolled across the casino lobbies with the type of confident swagger that men admired and women would swoon over. Boasting the triple threat of glamour, talent, and machismo, the glamorous stars attracted the big spending high rollers, as well as millions of other gamblers, to the glitzy, mob-owned casinos where they performed. Admirers flocked to Las Vegas, just for a mere glimpse of the famous crooners.

The Rat Pack aura was theirs, alone, and although it may have been artificially inflated, it was real in the hearts and minds of their fans. Their signature 'bad boy' image glamorized the image of drinking, gambling and womanizing – all the staples of Las Vegas.

Like the others, Sammy had no trouble living up to their audacious reputations, convincingly playing 'the swinger,' on a 24-hour basis. The stage was, literally, his home. So, pausing during a performance, for a drink, or a cigarette, was commonplace.

Over the years, the cultural impact of the iconic group would inspire fans of nearly every race and generation. The Rat Pack would remain a part of American culture, as witnessed in the ongoing celebration of its members in paintings, posters, and other mementoes.

Whether Sammy was performing professionally, or not, he loved being on center stage. In fact, the only thing that rivaled with his celebrity as a performer was his penchant for provoking controversy. Members of the paparazzi, who never grew tired of stalking him, covered each explosive episode of his love life, from his contentious affair with white actress, Kim Novak, during the late 1950's, to the death threats he received after marrying Swedish actress, May Britt.

In between the two, was his shot-gun-styled wedding with a black entertainer named Loray White. It was a hastily arranged, paid nuptial, which was forced on Sammy by a studio-connected mobster, who'd threatened him with violence if he continued the Novak affair. Since Davis wanted to keep his one remaining eye, he immediately grabbed his little black book to find a wife.

In 1970, Sammy was married again, this time to Altovise Gore, and the couple would become Hollywood's version of Bonnie and

Clyde. They were notorious for hosting numerous gatherings where the phrase, 'anything goes,' could have easily been coined. Their sprawling Beverly Hills home was the scene of parties that catered to aficionados of heavy drinking, experimental sex – especially wife swapping and orgies – and the flagrant use of drugs.

Although, Altovise, herself, was a professional dancer, and had performed with Sammy on various stages, somewhere along the way, she'd lost a strong sense of herself. Living with Sammy could be overwhelming; for a man with a small physique, his persona would cast a huge shadow.

Following their marriage, Altovise continued to appear in Sammy's shows, at least, until the period when entertainer, Katherine McKee, replaced her, both, under the stage lights of Sammy's productions and under the silk sheets of his bed. Altovise and Sammy's 'open marriage' allowed Katherine to assume the role of Sammy's 'road wife,' but it would also contribute to Altovise's long and painful battle with alcohol. Despite the complicated, and sometimes degrading nature of their union, she would always call Sammy her hero. After all, he was like an open wallet.

During the height of his career, Sammy, literally, made millions each year, but, unfortunately, made an art of spending considerably more. Back during his heyday – when the money was good and the loans were quick – he got away with it. After all, there was always another show to cover his debts.

Sammy, who had extravagant tastes, shared his indulgent lifestyle with Altovise, who, like her husband, shopped with almost reckless abandon. From luxurious furs and exquisite jewels, to a fleet of customized and exotic cars, Sammy tried to quench their every desire.

The years of hard living and reckless spending would eventually catch up to the star. His business and investment ventures were plagued with mismanagement. A troubling pattern existed in which Sammy had been underpaid by various recording studios, and he'd signed contracts which offered less than favorable terms. There were even instances in which he'd failed to secure the master recordings of his own songs.

Having lived far beyond his means, when Sammy died of throat cancer in 1990, he left to his wife an estate that was embroiled in a huge legal and financial crisis. With over $5 million owed to the IRS, alone, Altovise faced a tax lien that, at the time, was the highest in the country. The glamorous and privileged life she'd known for twenty years was now over.

Altovise was ill-prepared to accept the sobering realities of her new life, especially when the IRS seized the Davis estate, selling their twenty-two room mansion and auctioning their most precious possessions. She was equally unprepared for the cold rejection of some of their oldest friends, especially Bill Cosby, who'd been one of Sammy's closest buddies.

After all, when Sammy was battling cancer, he made one of his last T.V. appearances on *The Cosby Show,* and on the day of Sammy's funeral, Cosby was an honorary pallbearer. To memorialize him, Bill wore Sammy's initials on his clothing during the following season of his show. It was the type of moving, Cosby-like gesture for which he was so famous.

However, while Bill donned Sammy's initials in public, behind the scenes, he had a very different attitude. Altovise later confided in me that she'd been desperate for help, but when she'd reached out to Bill, she'd been shocked by his indifference. "He never helped me," she said, her voice still filled with pain. A friend had also called Bill on her behalf, but she claimed that he'd never even called back.

In the following seasons, Altovise would quietly disappear from the public, and her whereabouts would be a mystery for many years, at least, up until 2004, when she first resurfaced in Sarasota, Florida. A cloud of questions still remained, though, regarding the years when she was seemingly 'missing,' and the final outcome of the Davis estate.

A few months later, in 2005, a friend would introduce me to Altovise, to help write her autobiography. I welcomed the new assignment with the intention of, first, learning all I could about her amazing life. In my efforts to understand Altovise's struggle – the pressures of her marriage and the magnitude of her debt – I began to research Sammy's career and their unconventional marriage.

I was struck by the cruel dichotomy in Altovise's life. I was lunching with a woman who'd entertained some of the world's most famous celebrities. She'd once lived in a sprawling Beverly Hills mansion, where, parked out front, was a Rolls-Royce bearing her name on its plate. That day, however, she would return to a cramped little apartment down the street from my community and actually need a ride to get home.

Altovise and I found that we shared a passion for creating children's stories, an interest which began to consume most of our conversations. We became increasingly drawn to the idea of collaborating on stories that might impact the lives of teens, especially future artists. This was ideal, because Altovise wasn't ready to discuss the sensitive nature of her marriage, which was controversial, to say the least. Nor, was she forthcoming about the last 'missing' years of her life. In fact, a frightening new problem was developing, and she couldn't speak about this, either.

I paused the work that I'd begun on Altovise's autobiography, because her life was far more complex than it had first appeared. She was struggling with a great deal more than just a mountain of debt and a Smirnoff bottle, stashed inside her Louis Vuitton. Behind her radiant smile was a woman facing, still another crisis.

Altovise wasn't exactly homeless when she was later evicted from her Sarasota apartment, but her tenuous situation became something close to perilous.

To make bad matters worse, rumor had it that two men were stealing her belongings, raiding her bank accounts and sponging off what was left of Sammy's estate. For some reason, Altovise believed that she'd found herself a hero in one of the men. When they entered a business partnership – though it was heavily tilted in their favor – she'd believed that her rags-to-riches-to-rags ordeal was over.

Unfortunately, when Altovise signed over the control of Sammy's estate, she unwittingly opened up Pandora's Box.

Being a quiet and soft-spoken writer, I never wanted to be pulled into a messy legal battle, especially since Altovise, initially, wanted to keep this part of her life private. So, even when their arrangement went sour, I managed to refrain from getting involved, that is, until February 2007, on the unforgettable evening of the Academy Awards.

# 1

## THE MEETING

*March 8, 2005*
*Sarasota, Florida*

The day had arrived. After several weeks of postponements, my friend, Lisa Hollar, and I were finally meeting with Altovise Davis at a casual Chinese restaurant not far from my home. As I drove down Lockwood Ridge, I wondered why I felt so nervous. One would think that I'd never met, nor worked with, anyone who was famous. I had, but this was very different.

Altovise was the widow of the legendary Sammy Davis, Jr., the Rat Pack star who was often called "The World's Greatest Entertainer." Throughout my entire life, his name was as recognizable as Frank Sinatra's and Elvis Presley's. Now, there was talk about a major movie about his life. What intrigued me most was the fact that, after Sammy's death and the firestorm of legal and financial calamities that toppled his estate, Altovise had practically vanished from the public. Her whereabouts were a mystery for several years, and now she was here in Sarasota. In fact, at the time, we all lived near one another in communities located just off University Parkway on the northern border of the city. So the low-keyed restaurant was an ideal spot to meet.

Admittedly, it was my custom to run a few minutes late, and such was the case that day, despite the meeting's close proximity to my house. As I rushed to the door of Cang Tong III, I paused a moment to take a deep breath.

Scuffling was not acceptable; I needed to look calm and collected. As expected, Lisa and Altovise were already seated at a table when I arrived, and immediately turned around to greet me when I strolled in. Lisa, with a penetrating stare, began the introductions.

"Altovise, this is my friend, Pam."

"How are you?" asked Mrs. Davis, extending her hand.

"It's good to finally meet you," I said.

Altovise looked nothing like the woman I'd envisioned. I was expecting a lovely septuagenarian, since Sammy – were he still alive – would have been nearly eighty years old.

She was, however, one of those amazing ladies - I call them phantoms - who seem to escape the aging process. She was a former dancer, and even while seated, it was obvious she was in great shape. Blessed with amazing genes, her soft brunette hair showed no signs of grey, and her wrinkleless brown skin appeared as soft as a baby's. Was she fifty-something? I wondered. Or, was she in her early sixties?

I smiled, hoping the surprise didn't register on my face, and when Altovise smiled back I felt a surge of relief. Once comfortably seated, I asked how she felt about relocating to Sarasota, and we immediately began a lively conversation.

None of us dared to compare the Tampa Bay Area to Los Angeles, but we agreed that Sarasota was certainly blessed with extraordinary qualities. The long list of assets ranged from the natural beauty of its emerald bay and sugar-colored beaches to the exciting architectural themes that complemented the tropical landscapes.

At the heart of the city, and its quaint shops along Main Street, was a festive aura that permeated from a cornucopia of cultural amenities. In addition to hosting numerous theaters, it was the hometown of the famous Ringling Bros. and Barnum & Bailey Circus and the Sarasota Ballet. These qualities were complemented by the treasures found along the Keys – the magnificent islets located just a bridge away – and beckoned, not only tourists, but patrons of the arts and a vast array of talented artists.

"I want to open a dance school here," said Altovise, in a slightly theatrical tone. Lisa, who was helping her find a suitable building, nodded and said the city was perfect for the school she had in mind.

"I think you're right," I replied, considering the Ringling School of Art & Design and the numerous programs devoted to youth. "There's a great deal of talent here."

"I'm going to call it 'Bojangles,' after my husband," said Altovise, anxious to get my response.

"Good choice," I said, recalling that I'd once seen Sammy perform 'Bojangles,' on TV. Who could forget his signature dance routine? I'd always thought it was his own special tribute to the tap dancer, Bill Robinson, and agreed it was a good name.

I thought it was also a good time to approach the topic we'd delayed discussing for several weeks. I'd never been pushy but I realized it was entirely possible to have a pleasant lunch, chat about amazing people, and never get to the reason why we'd gathered. It was my place to take the initiative.

Altovise was looking for someone to assist with her autobiography. Being a writer and a single mom, I was excited about the opportunity and wanted to be up-front about what I could offer. I wondered, though, if I appeared professional enough. Gone were the days when I rushed to interviews in starchy black suits. Friends joked that I'd lived in Honolulu too long, for my daily uniforms typically consisted of one of three styles: a Hawaiian muumuu; a long Indian skirt; or a casual jumper. Although it may have been risky to appear so dowdy, I'd chosen a slightly faded jean jumper to wear that day.

It felt right, however, because Altovise was just as casual. Dressed in comfortable slacks and a top, she sat back and listened as I briefed her on my background. She was so low-profile, in fact, that the only hint that she was, indeed, Mrs. Davis, was the impressive gem she donned on her ring finger. Her manner, friendly and unassuming, made her so indistinguishable that a neighbor had flatly refused to believe she was Sammy's wife. When Altovise first identified herself, the woman had actually laughed uncontrollably, assuming that she was joking. From that day on, the neighbor would howl hysterically whenever the two encountered one another. Amused at first, I later wondered how many times Altovise had faced this reaction.

I'd had a broad range of experiences, which I mentioned, and I'd recently completed my first book. Reaching over the table, I handed her a copy of it.

"It's really about a spiritual journey," I advised her, wanting to discuss my Christian beliefs without imposing them on her. I knew from experience that this could pose a thorny issue, not merely because of my interest in ministry, but because Altovise may have wondered if my beliefs would influence my perspective. If so, there would naturally be one big question: Was I objective enough to be a ghostwriter for her book? After all, she'd have to feel comfortable in confiding in me, and I, in turn, would have to feel comfortable handling her personal confessions. Although, I was still learning about her, I realized there were some sensitive issues we'd have to tackle. Regardless, my responsibility was to help Altovise express herself, openly and honestly, and I needed to do this without judging or forming any strong opinions.

I glanced across the table at Altovise, knowing she was probably wondering if I was up to the task. Quite frankly, I wondered, myself, as she politely nodded and I continued to discuss my interests.

Since this was our first meeting, I tried to keep it relatively informal. There was no need to overwhelm her with too any details, especially since, everything depended on whether we could work well together. I wasn't going to bog down the conversation with stories about my life when I was more interested in hearing about hers.

Hopefully, there would be future opportunities to share more about my work. In the meantime, she could read about my adventures, or misadventures, in my book. Still, I do recall telling her that I'd attended Howard University around the same time that Lisa was there.

I glanced over at Lisa, marveling at the fact that we never met during those years.

Altovise thought quietly for a moment. I assumed she was considering my work experience and questioning the level of my skills.

"My husband always took good care of me," she finally said, sampling the seafood dish the waitress placed between us. "I never had to worry or do anything for myself. Everything was always provided for me."

"Oh," I responded, nodding as though I'd had comparable experiences. I gazed at Lisa who silently smirked. Her own sweet hubby had recently pressured her to get a job.

"It must be nice," snickered Lisa. "Yeah," I agreed, trying not to laugh.

We'd ordered a variety of Chinese dishes, and although the food looked sensational and the aroma was enticing, I'd just begun a week-long fast, so I settled for a bowl of tofu-vegetable soup. As we ate, Altovise's words began to replay in my head and they naturally led to several questions.

There was no doubt about the validity of her comments, for she'd once enjoyed a very affluent lifestyle. In fact, Altovise, or Alto, as friends called her, enjoyed the wealth and glamour associated with being the third Mrs. Sammy Davis, Jr. for some twenty years. She transitioned from relative obscurity as a backup dancer to being the doting wife of the man she idolized, and she played an extraordinary role in Sammy's life. Being partnered with a famous celebrity, however, was undoubtedly a mixed bag of blessings and curses.

Keeping up with Sammy would have been a formidable challenge for any woman. He was, in a word, a phenomenon – a twenty-four hour, luminous star who, like the Las Vegas casinos where he performed, was virtually always "on."

I studied Altovise's face, trying to image life with an American icon. Multi-talented and driven like a rocket, it was common for Sammy to sing, dance, and impersonate other celebrities, then fire off jokes with equal degrees of spontaneity and wit. He didn't just delight audiences; his charisma and command of the stage would mesmerize fans of every age and race. Should anyone, then, have been surprised that he was also a musician and delivered rousing performances in Broadway plays, movies, and variety shows?

Was there anything Sammy couldn't, or wouldn't, try? I wondered. Where had so much talent come from? Altovise would be delighted to shed some light on these questions. She mentioned, more than once, that Sammy started performing when he was only three or four years old, sacrificing the normal childhood experiences – including school – for a career in vaudeville. During those early years, when he first began "hoofing" with his father and Will Mastin, they passed him off as a midget. Young Sammy would perform for many years with the Will Mastin Trio, eventually becoming the main breadwinner. Since they travelled much like gypsies, his only true home, and virtual playground, was the stage. Years later, it would seem like the place where he felt most comfortable. In fact, many would say, whether Sammy was on stage or off, he was always performing.

How had Altovise handled such a human dynamo? True, she'd been an entertainer, herself, but was she really prepared to keep up with him? At first, their courtship and marriage must have been a dazzling sort of whirlwind. However, after the excitement of the honeymoon season, she must have confronted the pressures that came with the tremendous new challenges, some with the force of land mines. How had she adapted to Sammy's hectic schedules and varied social life? Then, there were the nuances of maneuvering around Hollywood and Las Vegas. And, of course, there were the other women in his life, and the intrusive presence of the media.

It was like a love-hate relationship, the strange chemistry between Sammy and the media. During the height of his career, the paparazzi and their cameras, were inescapable, for, if anything rivaled Sammy's enormous talent and his prolific career, it was his flair for inciting controversy. This was partially due to his unconventional lifestyle. Whether he baited the press, or not, he made an art of making the headlines, and this trait became key to his persona.

While, he applied much of his energy toward breaking racial barriers during the early years of his career, by the 1970s, no celebrity swayed wider than Sammy when it came to enjoying a swinger's life. In many minds, he embodied the essence of Rat Pack machismo, making him a viable contender for a hedonist's poster child. He sometimes appeared to be everywhere all at once, from his songs heard on the radio, to the TV sitcoms. Sammy's high visibility made his face one of the most recognized throughout the world. Often, the most vivid images were those of him positioned beside a beautiful woman.

It was Sammy's involvement with a few alluring beauties that led to the most spellbinding episodes in his life. Interestingly, it was his third and last marriage that managed to fly just under the radar detectors, at least, for a while.

Altovise Gore Davis, perhaps the most mysterious, and misunderstood, of the many women who frequented Sammy's life, would outlast all the others, defying expectations in the famous, but fickle, circles in which they mingled. Sammy, who had a long-standing reputation for courting glamorous blonds, had somehow – and for some extraordinarily reason – suddenly made an abrupt change. Who was this unknown dancer, the first black woman with whom he'd freely chosen to spend his life? Many were taken aback by their discrete marriage ceremony, and when the union lasted and the couple defeated the seven-year-itch by renewing their vows, observers mused over the success of their marriage. Or was it a success, at all?

During the 1970s the couple gained notoriety for not only hosting some of the most lavish parties in Hollywood – but for establishing spending habits so extravagant that they reportedly depleted the millions that Sammy earned. They were known to mingle with royalty, statesmen and famous celebrities, and from these frolics were stories of heavy drug use, drinking, and various sexual exploits that earmarked theirs as an open marriage. Rumors about their financial and personal indiscretions would eventually snowball into something just short of a public scandal.

Although many years had passed, I still recalled a few of the stories about Sammy's death, but mostly tidbits I'd heard on the evening news. Back then, I regarded Sammy as a superstar from my parents' era. I was more interested in Prince and Michael Jackson. But, I was left with the vague impression that the Davis estate was encumbered, and the couple had ended up owing money to someone.

The staggering degree of debt, in fact, made history. When Sammy died, he reportedly owed the IRS over $5 million, a figure which eventually swelled to approximately $7 million, and represented the largest tax lien in the country's history. Altovise would inherit this colossal bill, as well as others, which initialed a financial and legal nightmare that led to the loss of their home and the auctioning of their personal belongings. Yes, the swinging times had ended with Sammy's death, but like most people, I never knew what followed.

Fifteen years had passed, and the greatest enigma still surrounded the fate of Altovise, who, like a fine vapor, had practically disappeared for much of that time. Many wondered, even within their social circles, what had happened to her.

It was in December 2004 when Lisa first phoned with the news. Altovise Davis was in Sarasota. Mutual friends had introduced them, and Lisa was assisting her in efforts to open a dance school in the city.

Lisa paused a moment, gathering momentum for a bigger announcement. "Pam, there's something else." she continued. "Altovise wants to write a book about her life, and she's looking for a writer to help her." Before I could utter a word, she added, "And I told her all about you and the book you wrote. She wants to meet you!"

There was a scream building up inside, but I managed to calmly reply, "Sure, I'd be happy to."

Lisa suggested that I come to her home for dinner, where she'd arrange an introduction. Altovise was traveling, but we'd get together within the next few weeks. The timing seemed perfect, as I was just finishing a project for an independent producer who was trying to pitch a new T.V. show for kids. He'd needed two sample episodes and a proposal, and the package was nearly complete. Since it was the first time I'd written anything for television, I'd devoted months to learning the new format. An old friend who was established in the industry – at Disney, in fact – provided the scripts to study and the screenwriting software to use. I'd also read various books, and it all amounted to a crash course in scriptwriting, children's programming, and character development. Still, I felt ready to switch back to the mindset required to write an autobiography.

"Fine," I thought. "Bring it on!"

Several weeks passed, however, and when I spoke with Lisa again, her tone was noticeably different. The enthusiasm in her voice was re-placed with concern and some degree of confusion. Something had gone wrong, but she wasn't expressing it openly.

"When will I meet Altovise?" I asked. Lisa's reply was vague and noncommittal, so I decided to drop the subject. When another few weeks passed, I assumed Altovise had found another writer.

In late February, however, Lisa called to tell me that Altovise was back in town and she'd asked about meeting me. Lisa explained that Altovise had been busy trying to arrange a commercial project with Natalie Cole. Now, she had some time to talk. Was I still interested?

"Are you kidding?" I laughed.

The waitress brought a small dish of fortune cookies, along with the check, but we were so engrossed in conversation, we barely no-ticed them.

Altovise was in a nostalgic mood. "You know, I was going with a doctor when I first started dating Sammy," she disclosed.

"Really?" I responded.

"But, of course, I ended up marrying Sammy," she continued, smiling.

I looked at the women seated across from me, and realized they'd shared something similar in their pasts.

Years before, when Lisa was single and living in Washington, D.C., she'd also dated a prominent physician. While they were vaca-tioning in Egypt, they stayed at a swanky hotel in Cairo. The facility also housed permanent residences, one of which was owned by the famous movie star, Omar Sharif. During their stay, the couple met and befriended the actor, and he soon invited them to dine as his guests.

Lisa, who'd planned an extensive tour of the ancient city, couldn't wait to begin their sightseeing trip. Her boyfriend, however, envisioned a vacation almost solely devoted to rest and relaxation. This presented a dilemma.

In his most charming manner, however, Sharif suggested a solution to their stalemate. He offered to be Lisa's personal escort while her friend enjoyed the hotel's amenities. The physician thought it was a gallant gesture. After all, it represented a once-in-a-lifetime opportunity for an American woman. How could he deprive Lisa of that? So, believing that Sharif's motives were entirely innocent, he took him up on the offer.

In assuming that Sharif's motives were virtuous, he couldn't have been more naive. Although Lisa was young, she was a very alluring woman whose smooth brown skin, jet black hair, and striking blue eyes, often engendered the memory of a younger, but permanently tanned, Elizabeth Taylor.

As I thought of this, I glanced at Lisa, again. It still struck me as odd that I didn't recall seeing her at Howard during the late 1970s. Back then, she was Lisa Roberts, and as photos confirmed, she was an unforgettable beauty. Elizabeth Taylor may have starred in the epic film, *Cleopatra*, but if anyone possessed the exoticism of an Egyptian queen, it was Lisa, and this didn't escape the attention of a number of other famous men.

When Sharif began to make advances, Lisa was both flattered and terrified. What was she to do? Although the actor had aged since he'd first burst onto the international scene, he was still attractive and extremely seductive. Unsure of how to proceed, she made an urgent call for help. Clutching the phone, she waited for what seemed like hours. Back in Chicago, her mother, a conservative Christian woman, had always preached in favor of abstinence. She'd often served as Lisa's sounding board, the trustee to her inner conscience. If advice was ever needed, it was certainly now.

So, Lisa braced herself as she awaited a parent's true words of wisdom. The minutes continued to pass uncomfortably. Then, from thousands of miles away, Lisa finally heard her mother's commandments, echoed almost instantly by an aunt standing nearby. Their instructions were short and to the point: "Do him!"

We all have days when the earth seems to stand still, and perhaps this was one of Lisa's, because she was definitely stunned. Still, the freedom to act sometimes prompts us to actually pull in the reins. Although she'd received the green light, Lisa said she restrained herself. In fact, in an act of chivalry, Sharif decided to do the same. He feared that, due to Lisa's young age, she was probably too vulnerable to get involved in an affair. They opted for a platonic relationship.

The story still made me chuckle, for those two ladies weren't the only members in Sharif's undying fan club. I, too, once suffered from a crush on the star, and when I spotted a photo of him embracing Lisa, I loudly exclaimed, "He was mine, first!"

Sammy Davis, Jr., unlike Sharif, wasn't deterred by the age difference between Altovise and himself. Although she was considerably younger – some eighteen years – they began a serious relationship which eventually led to marriage.

Turning my attention back to Altovise, I realized she was still a beautiful woman, and it was easy to see what attracted Sammy to her. She had a unique way of looking at you as though you were the most interesting person she'd ever met. She had a theatrical presence and her eyes glistened with a whimsical quality that seemed much like that of a child. In fact, I'd later believe that it was her youthful countenance that had served as her refuge, an inner source of strength. It wasn't that she lacked maturity, or sophistication; on the contrary, she was extremely savvy, and yet, her qualities seemed purposely understated.

"What a charming woman," I later told Lisa.

One of the highlights of our meeting was a discussion surrounding a documentary about Sammy's life.

"I'm one of the producers," Altovise told me, ". . . along with Burt Boyar, the author who's written a few books about Sammy. I'm still gathering the photos we're going to use."

"When will it be broadcasted?" I asked.

"Probably in October," she replied.

"Wouldn't that be a wonderful time to launch your book?" I suggested. "With all the interest the show's going to generate."

Altovise and Lisa both agreed, and there was a growing sense of excitement as we discussed the possible scenario.

Also on the horizon were at least two major biopics about Sammy's life and Altovise had basically endorsed one of the films, though she wasn't enthralled with the actor who was considered for the role.

"He just doesn't favor Sammy in any way," she said, adding, "I'm going to be involved in producing this, as well."

The multi-faceted actor Ben Vereen, had expressed strong interest in playing Sammy's father, and since he and Altovise were good friends, she felt favorable about this.

With so much going on, I wondered how Altovise would balance all these projects, and still have time to work on her book. I questioned her about what she wanted to accomplish. She didn't hesitate a moment.

"I want to write about the last year I spent with Sammy," she said, and with a slightly lower voice, added, "And what happened, afterwards."

Altovise seemed anxious to set the record straight about a number of events that had taken place, and as I listened, I began to envision her story. It would be an inspiring memoir that spoke of triumph over adversity. I was charmed by her enthusiasm and captivated by the nature of the work still ahead of her. How thrilling it would be to play even a small role in helping her accomplish her goals. What an incredible blessing, I thought.

"Maybe you'd like to use flashbacks." I suggested. "You know, go back to special moments you shared, like your favorite holidays, your engagement, and wedding... events that recapture the nature of your relationship."

She nodded, agreeing that it would be helpful. I also recommended that she get a tape recorder and keep a pad with her at all times. Then, she could record the memories as they came back to her. Thanking me, she agreed to get them.

It was too soon to expect Altovise to reach a decision about working with me, but since there had been very warm and receptive vibes between us, I felt comfortable with the prospect of writing her book. In fact, our meeting couldn't have been more upbeat. Well, there had been one sobering moment, when I asked Altovise about their children. Had I done a little research, I would have approached this topic more delicately.

"Well, I have three wicked step-children..." Altovise began, pretending to bite her lip. "And one nice one."

Laughing slightly, Altovise said she was just joking, but she stuttered when she attempted to actually describe their relationships. I saw her discomfort, and knew it was my cue to drop the subject.

I'd later learn that Sammy fathered one child with May, his second wife, and it was his daughter named Tracey. Later, they adopted two boys, Mark and Jeff. For many years, Altovise and her stepchildren had a rocky relationship. As time passed, the boys eventually accepted her. However, Tracey, who liked to call her "Alpo," never seemed to adjust. There remained a great deal of resentment between them.

Altovise recalled one incident, in particular, which took place when Tracey was still very young. She was visiting her father in London, and according to Altovise, the child was so difficult to handle that "we sent her home."

In 1996, when Tracey published a book about her father, she apparently recalled some equally unpleasant memories, and didn't hesitate to write some uncomplimentary passages about her stepmom.

I'd also later learn that the "nice one" Altovise referred to, was the son that she and Sammy had later adopted. His name was Manny, and he was then in the armed services, and stationed in Iraq. She beamed with pride as she spoke of him, so I hesitated before I approached the next question.

"Aren't you nervous about the war in Iraq?" I inquired.

"No," she responded.

Like many optimistic Americans that year, Altovise was full of confidence in Manny's role there.

It was obvious that, when it came to family matters, Altovise felt more comfortable talking about her own mother, Mrs. Altovise Gore, who was then still living in New York. Elderly and ailing, she'd recently been injured in a fall and was convalescing in a nursing facility.

"So you're named after your mother," I said, commenting on how unusual the name was.

"It means higher vision," she said.

Altovise intended to take over her mother's care, which was part of her motivation for moving to Florida. "I'm going to bring her down here," she said, "where it's warmer and healthier."

I could easily relate, as I'd moved to Sarasota with my daughter and parents for similar reasons. I'd had a long battle with health problems, including an ongoing war with arthritis after undergoing nine hip surgeries. My parents were elderly, and had several health issues of their own. We'd weighed the options. We could try to tough it out in Connecticut or seek a healthier life in Florida. After a brutal winter in 2000, we knew the answer.

"Of course, I'm still looking for a house," Altovise stressed.

I glanced at Lisa who was trying to help her. She gazed back at me, her eyebrows arched with some annoyance. It didn't surprise me. Lisa had recently mentioned the enormous amount of time she'd invested in trying to get something accomplished, and yet, there was little progress. Like the building for the school, there had been no decision on a house. I knew Lisa was frustrated, so I didn't dawdle on the subject.

Surprisingly, the most engaging part of our conversation revolved around an interest that we unexpectedly shared in common. When I mentioned writing a proposal for a children's TV show, Altovise's eyes lighted up. She was so excited that she immediately turned to try to find something.

"You know what…" she began, reaching inside her Louis Vuitton bag, "I'm writing a story for children, myself." She rummaged inside the huge pocketbook, searching for something, but apparently without success. "I've got the disk… somewhere."

"I'll find it," she said, resolutely. "And let you see it, next time."

"I look forward to it," I replied, and we both smiled at each other.

A strong connection began at that moment, only I didn't realize its significance until much later. We actually planted a seed of friendship, which was based on the passion we shared for telling children's stories. This discovery, which took place within such a short timeframe, would have an amazing impact on the path ahead of us. It's odd, how life offers the most intriguing twists when you least expect them.

# 2

## GETTING TO KNOW YOU

*March 2005*
*Sarasota, Florida*

Altovise didn't like to get up too early, so we'd made arrangements to meet around 1:00 p.m. The Tuscany was located just down the street from Palm Aire, where I lived, so it was convenient for me to pick her up. I was actually surprised that she lived so close by, and when I glanced in the phone directory, she was on Medici Court. The attractive apartment complex had always drawn my attention, with its graceful Italian statues and artful landscaping. So, I couldn't wait to visit her. I imagined that the interior designs would be just as elegant as the entrance suggested.

In some ways, I felt hesitant, and almost apologetic, about driving her around in my car. It was an old Ford I'd bought from Rent-A-Wreck, and I'd grown attached to it because it was reliable. However, I didn't relish the idea of fetching Altovise in such a clunker and as I circled the drive at the Tuscany's entrance, I wondered how she'd react to it.

Within a few moments, I spotted the tennis court that Altovise said was on the right, and it meant that I was near her building. Her address was 6051 Medici Court. After parking the car, I walked past an attractive courtyard and soon found her unit. I knocked hard on the door and waited.

After several minutes, I knocked again and stepped back to reexamine the number. It was Apartment #103, so unless I'd written down the wrong address, I was at the right place. Glancing around the open square, I noticed a large, tiered water fountain in the midst of an elaborate pattern of shrubbery. The atmosphere was so serene that I wondered if residents ever sat on the benches to read or to soak up the peaceful aura.

Why hadn't anyone answered the door? I wondered. Wasn't it the right place, and the right time? I considered leaving and calling Altovise sometime later that day. Perhaps she'd taken a nap and couldn't hear the knock. I'd try once more.

To my relief, the door finally opened and there stood Altovise, smiling radiantly. She welcomed me in and I paused for a moment, because the apartment seemed so dark. The small living room was modestly furnished and most of the lighting was provided by the slider to the lanai. The walls were unadorned, giving the room a sterile feeling, but I remembered that the place was merely a temporary landing spot and not intended to be a real home.

As we talked, I noticed that, although no portraits graced the walls, numerous photos were stacked on the dining room table. Altovise, who must have followed my eyes, seemed pleased to lead me to them.

"You certainly have a lot of pictures," I said.

Picking up a few, she walked closer to me.

"Look at this one," she said, handing it to me.

The photo was taken of Sammy when he was only about four years old, but already a full-time entertainer. He was completely made up in minstrel attire, and it looked like a poster from the vaudevillian era. That's when Altovise mentioned that Sammy's father had passed him off as a midget. I gazed a long time at the image, because something about the picture actually haunted me. Sammy's young face – though painted in black – held a deep, solemn, sage-like wisdom. To me, he looked very sad.

In stark contrast was the proud smile that now stretched across Altovise's face. "You know, Sammy started performing when he was only three," she reminded me. "So, he didn't get to go to school like other kids."

"Wow!" I replied, reflecting on the child labor laws. "What an experience that must have been."

I considered the magnitude of the changes since then, and how today's young performers could have personal tutors or choose to attend public and private schools.

"And this one?" I asked, spotting a portrait of Sammy and Altovise.

"Oh, yes," she remarked, pulling it out. It was a lovely picture, taken early in their marriage. Sammy was sporting a neat Afro, which brought back memories of the seventies, and Altovise's young face was framed with bangs.

I noticed that she now preferred to pull her hair back in a ponytail or a twist. Apart from that, however, she looked much the same.

She showed me a photo of their son, Manny, and reminded me that he was in the armed services. I couldn't help but reiterate my feelings about war.

"Aren't you concerned about him being over there?" I asked. "Iraq is getting to be a dangerous place."

Altovise, however, seemed convinced that it was the best option for Manny, at least, during that year. I was initially baffled by this, but then remembered that I'd witnessed this type of pride in other soldiers' parents. To them, it was more than a war; it was a campaign against terrorism. That season, Altovise's sense of patriotism was very strong.

Perhaps it rekindled memories that Sammy shared of his own army experiences. Or she could have recalled when she and Sammy traveled to Vietnam to perform for the soldiers fighting on the front lines. While there, Sammy had met with many servicemen, listened to their grievances, and upon his return, personally conveyed them to President Nixon. He'd been something like a representative for those men, and he relished that role.

"You know" she said, "When Manny was in school he was embarrassed whenever Sammy came to pick him up. He didn't want the other kids to see his car. Thought it was too flashy."

She peered at the photo with glowing admiration. I smiled too, as I gazed at the handsome youth, and wondered what it was like to have been their son.

"He really looks like Sammy," I said.

"Oh, no" Altovise sighed, "He's not Sammy's natural son. We adopted him."

"Oh," I replied, stunned. I thought he bore a strong resemblance to both of them.

Altovise mentioned that she had many photos taken at Sammy's funeral. "And there's a movie of it, if you want to see it," she added. Then she began to mention some of the people who'd attended. I nodded, as the material seemed helpful.

Altovise briskly walked across the living room. "Pam, look at this."

She motioned for me to come and picked up a bobble head doll made in the likeness of her husband. "Isn't it cute?" she asked, joggling it. The oversized head began to pivot. "It's great, isn't it?"

I agreed and took a seat on the couch. At that moment I felt encouraged; we were moving in the right direction. These mementos would prove helpful in retracing the past, and since Altovise was comfortable in sharing them, we'd have great materials with which to work. To get a firm handle on it, we needed a specific game plan. I knew that, if we proceeded, I'd be responsible for doing the research and the actual writing of the book. Altovise would provide various details about her life, which I'd then transcribe and edit to prepare to write the manuscript.

"You should get a tape recorder," I suggested, once again. "Then, whenever you recall something important, you can immediately capture it. Just tape it."

Altovise liked this idea. Again, she enthusiastically agreed.

"And you should keep a pad nearby. Sometimes memories come back late at night, so keep it right by your bed."

"That's a great idea!" she replied. "I'll get them."

Much to my surprise, I heard footsteps in the hallway. I'd been under the impression that Altovise was alone. Her roommate, however, happened to be at home and soon emerged from a bedroom in the back.

When Tracey Helms entered the room, I turned and began to introduce myself, but she uttered only a few words to Altovise, and without looking at me, walked right back to her room. There was no introduction, no explanation, and no acknowledgment that she'd even appeared. I cringed when I heard the door close behind her. It was such a chilly encounter, I felt stunned. Then, I awkwardly turned back around. Strangely enough, when I glanced at Altovise, she registered no reaction. She simply smiled and resumed our conversation.

Lisa had already told me about Altovise's assistant, companion, secretary, or any of the other terms used to describe her position. Initially, Lisa was leery of the woman. She couldn't figure out her connection to Altovise. They were so un-alike, they seemed like the female version of the hit sitcom, **The Odd Couple.** Race was not as much a factor as the age difference between Altovise and this younger white woman. Then, there were the stark contrasts in their demeanor. While Altovise appeared reserved and had a strong sense of decorum, Tracey was more of an "in-your-face" type of woman who didn't hold much back. Tracey didn't seem to fit the image of someone Altovise would hire, especially to handle her correspondence. At first, this bothered Lisa so much that she wondered, "Why is she there?"

During recent weeks, however, something had changed. Lisa and Tracey had become very chummy. In fact, Tracey had started confiding in her like an old, trusted friend. Lisa in turn would share some of Tracey's stories with me, because, by then, something else was worrying her.

Altovise and Tracey had been in Sarasota for only five months, but a number of troubling situations had developed. Tracey was terribly unhappy with, both, their financial and living arrangements and was bitterly complaining about them. These complaints were aimed at Altovise's two managers, who'd allegedly promised to pay Tracey a substantial sum of money, which she'd never received. As she became more desperate, she began calling Lisa to express her growing anger. She also shared her fears that the men were taking advantage of Altovise.

On that first visit, I was already aware of these conversations, but I didn't think much about them. I dismissed Tracey's allegations, thinking that she, like any disgruntled employee, was merely sounding off and venting to anyone who'd listen. While I empathized with her frustration, I wasn't about to get caught up in the bickering, especially since it wasn't my business. Those were her issues. I was there to help Altovise write her story and I didn't think we'd be covering Tracey's list of complaints.

I was still curious, however, about why Tracey had been so cold and indifferent. Based on Lisa's descriptions, I expected her to be friendly, in a down-home sort of way. I wondered why she'd behaved so peculiarly. Perhaps she was merely curious about who was there, and came to the living room to check me out. Maybe she'd quickly decided that Altovise's visitor was just a "commoner," a local girl without any Hollywood credentials.

Lisa later concurred with this assessment. Tracey, who'd heard nothing about me that impressed her, was equally unmoved by my appearance. Admittedly, I didn't look hip, smooth, or chic. My dress code was so conservative that it seemed to scream: "BORING!"

As a result, Lisa said, "Tracey had a hard time taking you seriously."

Through her association with Altovise, Tracey had already met a number of well-known figures. So, my visit was rather lackluster, especially coming on the heels of recent visits from heavyweights from famous families. There was Natalie Cole, whom they'd met with when she was in town. I was told the singer and Altovise discussed the possibility of producing a commercial video project. No concrete plans were on the table, but the idea was to merge old film footage of Natalie's father – the legendary singer, Nat "King" Cole – with memorable film footage of Sammy.

Then there was Josh, whose name was dropped from time to time, but who remained a mystery to me for several weeks. Having never heard his last name, I had no idea who he was, only that he'd been the one who introduced Altovise to Lisa.

Altovise also mentioned that Dean Martin's daughter, Deana, was recently in town. She was promoting a book she'd just published, and Altovise spoke with her about her own ideas for a memoir.

"Deana gave me the name of her publishing house," said Altovise. "And a card for them."

"We might look into that," I responded, as it seemed like a promising lead.

In fact, there were numerous celebrities in Altovise's life, many of whom she still knew quite intimately. This was only natural, since she'd flourished in Hollywood circles for two decades. Even now, living somewhat like a refugee, Altovise carried a phone book that was a virtual directory of Who's Who in Tinsel Town. She was like a walking encyclopedia when it came to the history of entertainers. In fact, there were few people whom I'd asked her about that she hadn't known or met. Aside from her obvious connections to Frank Sinatra, and Sammy's other Rat Pack friends, she'd also hung out with Elvis Presley, Elizabeth Taylor, Michael Jackson, and scores of other legends. During Altovise's first year of marriage, Lucille Ball had actually taken the new bride under her wing. Such was the crowd that she'd long considered her own.

I was amazed that Altovise had insider's knowledge about newcomers to Hollywood. She knew details about the lives of people like Paris Hilton and Nicole Richie, this, despite her lengthy absence from their circles. Her own life, however, had become somewhat of a mystery, and Altovise mentioned that even Deana Martin had asked where she'd been, and of course, the five-million dollar question: How was she doing?

When I asked her where she'd been all those years, she hesitated a moment, then mentioned having spent some time in New York with her parents.

"But, most of the time," she said, "I was living in Pennsylvania with my uncle." Then she chuckled and told me she'd worked in a department store there. Other than that, she said very little.

I'd eventually learn more about those 'missing' years. In passages in Matt Birkbeck's *Deconstructing Sammy*, were details offered by Albert "Sonny" Murray, Jr., an attorney who represented Altovise and the Sammy Davis, Jr. Estate from 1994 to 2001. He'd negotiated with the IRS to settle much of the estate's outstanding debt and went after companies that still owed them royalty payments.

Murray's family owned and managed the Hillside Inn in the Marshall's Creek area of the Pocono Mountains. It was a popular resort that catered to blacks for many years. Altovise stayed in a room within one of the thirty-six homes that were also located on the property.

According to the writer, the "uncle" whom Altovise referred to was actually Calvin Douglas, a former coworker and friend of her father's.

As I looked at Altovise that day, something else occurred to me. Despite all the tragedies in her life, she still remained very polished. With Sammy's death, her whole world had ended. Although her surroundings were pleasant, they were extremely modest compared to her Beverly Hills estate. She'd had the very best of everything, which Sammy had taken great joy in providing.

Altovise met some of the world's most accomplished individuals, not only in the entertainment industry, but in science, business, and politics. She'd been a guest at the White House, and rubbed shoulders with the scions of famous royal families. These days, she lived a very quiet, almost reclusive life. I wondered how she'd handled what many would agree were incomprehensible losses.

Curiosity led to questions that dated back still further, to the days when Altovise Joanne Gore was a young, aspiring dancer and actress. What led her to embark on such an intriguing life? Like Sammy, she was a native New Yorker, only Sammy was born in Harlem and Altovise was raised in Brooklyn. Some cities leave distinctive marks on people, and the magical aura of the theater district may have left an unshakable trace of stardust on both of their lives.

Unlike Sammy, whose training had taken place right on the job, Altovise attended the School of Performing Arts (now known as

New York's High School of Performing Arts). From there, she carved out a promising career as a stage dancer and, later, performed on Broadway, which was no small accomplishment for a black woman in the 1960s. Her talent would eventually provide her with opportunities to travel and perform abroad. In fact, in 1968 she played the role of Sammy's sister in the London production of his hit show **Golden Boy.** That's where the two became close friends.

When I tried to imagine Altovise about thirty-five years younger, I couldn't help but envision a striking dancer with a dazzling presence. I was always struck by a special radiance that still shined when she smiled, this despite the difficult nature of her circumstances. Sammy, undoubtedly, noticed this too.

While some have speculated that Altovise was drawn to Sammy's fame, she once told me it was his keen wit that attracted her most. In many ways, he seemed bigger than life, and Altovise certainly idolized him. His glamorous lifestyle would have drawn any woman's attention, and often did. He wasn't extremely handsome, but few could resist his irrepressible charm, which made observers wonder – with so many women at his disposal – why he had such a penchant for Altovise. Unlike the countless other beauties who danced in and out of Sammy's life, Altovise would waltz in and stay for the duration.

One author suggested that their union was based on their mutual appreciation for extravagant living. Others believed it was Altovise's youth, beauty, and winsome manner. Sammy, who'd been divorced twice, said that he hoped she'd bring stability to his life, and "a refreshing breath of wholesomeness." Whether that dream was plausible or not, we may never know, but Sammy entered their union with that desire.

After their marriage, Altovise performed as a dancer in many of Sammy's nightclub acts and was often featured as the leggy show-girl who'd bring his drinks on stage. They made a stunning couple, though she was considerably taller, and he liked to show her off in fine clothes and expensive furs. Sammy encouraged Altovise to actively pursue her career. He wanted her to shine and nurture her own star status. So, when she expressed an interest in acting, he strongly supported her and purchased a building for a production company. To her credit, Altovise appeared in TV shows such as *Charlie's Angels*, and a few minor films, including *Kingdom of the Spiders* with *Star Trek's* William Shatner. She was also proud to advise me that she was still a member of the Academy of Motion Picture Arts and Sciences.

As we headed to lunch that day, I felt like someone strolling with royalty. I was so thrilled that, for a moment, I was somewhat light-headed. Sooner or later, however, I'd have to get serious about our direction, assuming we were headed in the same direction, so silently, I began to juggle a number of questions I wanted to ask. With each step, however, I grew more anxious.

When Altovise and I approached my car, an awkward feeling overtook me, and my confidence began to dwindle. I knew she'd once owned a personalized Rolls Royce, among other luxury cars, and I could only offer a ride in my dingy old Ford. In my mind, this seemed a cruel testimony to how far life's pendulum could sway. I imagined that, fifteen years earlier, Altovise had parked her own car at her Beverly Hills estate, where, on frequent occasions she'd hosted fabulous parties. Watching the famous guests who drove up their driveway would have made me feel giddy. That dazzling era now seemed as distant as the mythical days of Camelot.

One's perceptions are often clouded by their past experiences, and having read many fairy tales as a child, I tended to romanticize the events I witnessed. So, admittedly, I was in awe of Altovise and held a rather dreamy vision of her. Seemingly trapped in an inescapable role, she reminded me of a lost and forgotten queen, like Guinevere, only Sir Lancelot wasn't there to rescue her. Due to their debts to the IRS and various creditors, their castle was stormed and overtaken. Altovise was virtually exiled, forever, and had sought refuge in this new land. How devastating, I thought, to be banished from her home. What had she experienced on the other side of her fortress and the secured grounds of the Davis estate? What was it like, standing here, in the sobering aura of this small parking lot? It must have been anything but easy.

As I drove toward the restaurant, my thoughts lingered on Altovise's plight, and I wondered how she'd managed to survive. I'd heard of "rags-to-riches" stories, but rarely the reverse. She'd overcome, what many thought, were insurmountable odds. Certainly, this was the essence of her story, the most compelling message that she'd deliver.

I looked at her as she peered out the window, believing that her life's lessons would offer a heartwarming testimony. That's what people needed – inspiration. And who knew better than Altovise about experiencing devastating losses? The message in her book – and its all-important last chapter – would resonate with a message of triumph. Struggling single women, whose own fairy tales had gone awry, were looking for hope. I wasn't ashamed to admit that I was one of them. Being very spiritual, I felt that God had blessed me with a project that would have a real impact on people's lives. In my eyes, Altovise was a bona fide survivor, and her amazing story would rock the country.

# 3

## THE CHILDREN'S HOUR

*March 2005*
*Sarasota, Florida*

Altovise and I went to dinner one night at Johnny Carino's, an Italian restaurant which was then located on University Parkway. As we stepped through the doors, we were instantly greeted by the crooning voice of Sammy Davis, Jr.

"I can't believe it!" exclaimed Altovise, laughing. "I never go into a restaurant and hear his voice!"

I couldn't believe it, either, because I'd never been to Carino's when they weren't featuring Italian singers.

"Are you sure?" I asked, politely. Altovise was the man's wife and should have known best. But, then again, I'd been there several times, and each time noticed how strongly the rustic Tuscan atmosphere was accentuated by Italian music. Sammy was black, Jewish, and best friends with Frank Sinatra, but he wasn't Italian.

"It's a good omen," said Altovise, now glowing.

"Sure it's not Sinatra?" I asked.

"No," she said adamantly, "It's Sammy!"

At that, Altovise walked over to the hostess to confirm it. The girl, too young to have known of Sammy, had no idea of whose voice was featured. However, she promised to ask the manager when she got a chance. In the meantime, we were seated at a booth not far from the grill.

The place was busy that night, and the hostess never got back to us. This didn't bother Altovise, because our conversation was flowing, much like the music.

It was easy to be with Altovise, and I couldn't help notice the way she shined when out in public. Her eyes had a warm and whimsical look, as though she was awaiting something exciting to happen. I'd noticed this the first time we'd dined out. She seemed to appreciate the simply joy of exchanging smiles with strangers. In fact, she was very gracious to nearly everyone and would rush to open doors for others. No wonder people didn't suspect who she was. It was sometimes difficult for me to remember.

Altovise must have suddenly thought of the hostess and began to speak about how this generation really didn't know Sammy. She recalled meeting a teenager who couldn't relate to him at all. They happened to meet her one night in their hotel lobby, and the girl boldly told Sammy that she wasn't a big fan of his. The Davises invited the teen to talk with them up in their suite. They spent much of the evening together, and Sammy found that the youth had a one-sided impression of him. They eventually reached a meeting of the minds and they all became good friends. In fact, the couple stayed in touch with the young woman throughout the years.

"And Sammy paid for her college tuition," Altovise said.

"Is that right?" I asked, as she nodded.

"Yes, he was very generous."

Altovise was proud to say that the woman had established a very successful career and was then living in Washington D.C.

About that time, the waiter brought each of us a glass of wine and we continued to talk.

"You know, Sammy wanted me to urge young artists to get their education. It was very important to him," said Altovise. She reminded me that her husband began performing when he was only three or four.

"So, he never got a chance to go to school," she said. "And, he always regretted it."

Altovise looked a bit somber for a moment, but began to perk up again as she continued.

"Years later, he'd learned to read when he was in the army. Then he'd read everything. He'd quiz me about a president, and if I didn't know the answer he'd scold me, and say 'You went to school!'"

Altovise laughed as she recalled this.

"I'm planning to go to schools around the country," she said. "And lecture to students about the importance of getting their education."

She looked convicted about this, and informed me that it was one of the goals of the Sammy Davis, Jr. Foundation. Altovise thought this would be a great way to keep Sammy's legacy alive. I nodded and listened with great interest, as it all sounded very laudable. The problem was, I had a hard time imaging young kids being attentive. Altovise was very soft-spoken. So, I wondered how she'd grab and hold their attention. Ugly flashbacks returned of a substitute teaching experience, when I'd lost my voice from screaming all day. I wondered if kids would really listen to Altovise. Would they even care who her husband was?

"I'd be happy to help," I said, "If you need any ideas for your speeches."

Altovise looked like she genuinely welcomed my help and talked about a future gathering that she planned to attend.

We ordered fish, agreeing that the grouper looked good.

Meanwhile, another idea began to formulate, and during those moments, I began to consider it very carefully. Wasn't something else happening, here? We both wanted to have an impact on young people's lives. Altovise was trying to give speeches and write books, and I'd been dabbling in screenplays for television. We both loved children and dreamed of creating stories for them. Shouldn't we seek a way to do it together? Maybe, we could entertain kids while we taught them valuable lessons.

After I left Altovise that night, I was carrying more than just ideas. I was holding a disk she'd given me, containing two of the children's stories she'd begun. I couldn't wait to see them and shortly after I returned home, tried to pull them up on my computer. Unfortunately, though, I couldn't find them.

I phoned Altovise.

"Are you sure it's the right disk?" I asked, recalling how she'd fished for it in her bag that first day, but hadn't located it.

"Yes," Altovise insisted. "That's it."

The following day we drove to a business store to retrieve the material on one of their computers, but the clerk was unsuccessful. Undaunted, Altovise suggested that we call a friend in New York, the woman whose computer she'd actually used. As we headed toward her apartment I began to realize how important this was to her. She was determined for me to see her stories. In fact, it seemed to overshadow her interest in her own memoir.

Altovise phoned her friend, a neighbor of her mother's, but again, we'd reached a dead end. The woman said that the stories had been deleted. Feeling frustrated, Altovise handed me the phone, but there was nothing I could do except to thank the woman for checking.

During the days that followed, I'd feel confused about which way we should go. Altovise and I would meet several times a week, but we were spending less time discussing her life and more time sharing ideas about children's stories.

When we did discuss her past, it was usually limited to her most treasured memories. When it came to confronting difficult subjects, she tended to withdraw. I was a trained journalist, but I found it increasingly difficult to broach any sensitive topics. I wasn't sure that she was really strong enough to go back and face them. An even more daunting question began to surface: "Was I?"

"Alto," I'd say, coaxing as much as possible, "It's best for you to be open. Tell people about the realities of your life. Otherwise, you let others do it for you. No one expects you to be perfect. There's no one who is. But, when you address the things that happened, people will respect you for your courage."

Altovise would agree with me, but say very little.

That spring, we had four or five of these one-sided conversations, and the result was always the same. Altovise would dodge the topic of her past, and I'd end up avoiding any difficult questions, at least, until she felt more comfortable about answering them. This represented only one of the problems that delayed our work. The second issue involved the all-important message needed for her last chapter.

I believed that, to write a good autobiography, Altovise had to make a meaningful statement. While I was impressed by her strength and tenacity, I knew she needed to take the next step. After enduring so much loss, she had to finally be a winner. If she'd gained wisdom from her trials, now was the time to express it. In fact, her life needed to reflect this. Otherwise, she wasn't ready to share her story. Even if we began writing the first pages, we couldn't tackle the last chapter until she literally started a new chapter in her life. I felt encouraged, though, since Altovise was already approaching this juncture. Once she got her school off the ground, or published her children's books, she'd have a new career and a testament to her accomplishments.

# 4

## WHAT'S WRONG WITH THIS PICTURE?

*Late March 2005*
*Sarasota, Florida*

"Has Alto been drinking with you?" asked Lisa.

"What?" I responded, completely off guard. "What do you mean?"

Tracey, her roommate, had complained to Lisa that Altovise and I had been out a lot, and that she'd been drinking with me. Lisa informed me that Altovise wasn't supposed to have "even the slightest amount of alcohol." It was dangerous to her health.

Stunned, I sat on the side of my bed and listened. My thoughts raced back through the past few weeks, scanning my memory for any incidents that were questionable. We certainly hadn't been to any clubs or bars. We'd only ordered an occasional glass of wine with our dinners. But, that was innocent. I wasn't an enabler. So, why was Lisa questioning me like I was corrupting Altovise? She knew I wasn't a party girl. In fact, I had an almost non-existent social life. The only events I regularly attended were the monthly luncheons hosted by the Sarasota's Christian Women's Club. I was their financial coordinator, and committed a lot of time to handling the ticket money, banking and monthly reports. My haunts were the places where I took my daughter – to the local libraries and Barnes & Noble Bookstore. If I was guilty of anything, it was taking Altovise to the same sober places.

I could hear Lisa take a deep breath before she began to explain. Altovise had been battling with alcoholism for many years and it had affected her health so seriously that there had been instances when it was life-threatening. Tracey told Lisa that Altovise suffered from cirrhosis of the liver and her doctors imposed a zero tolerance policy when it came to liquor. She was not to have a drop of anything. Although Tracey was her friend, her primary role, as a companion, was to ensure that Altovise stayed sober. Lisa stopped short of telling me how the women actually met, but continued to stress the importance of monitoring Altovise's drinking. I listened without mentioning the restaurant incidents, but silently vowed to make an immediate adjustment.

After I hung up, I sat there awhile just thinking. Altovise's behavior had never hinted of any problems. She'd always appeared stable. In fact, she conducted the most engaging conversations. She never slurred her words, or lost command of her thoughts, or her footing, for that matter. I'd never noticed any change at all, but if drinking – even a glass of wine – endangered her health or sobriety, I'd do nothing to encourage it. So, from now on, I'd simply order water.

Tracey was very protective of Altovise, and this was probably out of altruistic motives as well as her personal ambitions. So, I began to understand why she was initially so wary of me. I can't say that we ever became close friends, but we were considerably more cordial toward one another. While I didn't quite grasp the dynamics of their friendship, I sensed that they shared a common bond of some sort. Since no one spoke of it, and even Lisa seemed in the dark, I had no idea of what initially brought them together.

Tracey Helms was a tall, plain-spoken, Oklahoman, who didn't seem to be fond of dresses or makeup. That first day, like many others, she was wearing pajama-looking pants and a tee-shirt. She didn't appear to have been to the neighboring beaches, because her skin was very pale. She was a registered nurse, although, I'm sure I wouldn't have guessed it. Beyond the Southwestern twang that immediately caught my ear, was her colorful use of Ebonics and four-letter words.

Tracey tried hard not to use them around me, because Altovise, in a humorous tone, had said: "You can't curse in Pam's car!" Tracey complied, but only because they often had no other ride. Although she was Caucasian, Tracey relished her command of street lingo, and would sometimes scold Altovise for sounding "like she's white." Heavy-handed as it was, Tracey's criticism didn't appear to offend her roommate, because Altovise merely laughed at the remark. They were a strange pair, and I was sure that there were no two women who could be more different.

By late March, I'd read a number of books and articles about Sammy, and knew much more about his unusual life with Altovise. It was well documented that both agreed to have an open marriage. It was also well-known that, since Sammy tended to do everything in excess, his boundless energy and ardent pursuit of happiness extended to the most intimate aspects of his personal life. He introduced his wife to a world that included almost reckless spending, numerous affairs, frequent orgies, and heavy indulgence in drugs and alcohol. While most couples enjoyed the privacy of their homes, and a sensual experience that was uniquely theirs, in Altovise's marriage, the warmth of exclusive intimacy would be the only luxury she couldn't have. Even the private chambers of their bedroom offered little, if any, sanctity.

Their lives were extremely controversial. A few authors listed details about the couple's sexual habits that were so graphic and explosive that they left little to the imagination. I began to wonder how many of the stories were true, and how many were simply exaggerated cases of sensationalism? I knew the one person who had all the answers, and yet, something stopped me from delving too deep. My old journalism professors would have been disappointed, but frankly, there were some questions I just couldn't ask.

Whether I addressed them, or not, the questions kept popping up, and with them, a whole new set of issues. Was I the best writer for this gig? I wondered. I tried to suppress a growing fear, but I wondered what I was really getting into.

Through the years, a wide range of commentary was published on Altovise, some of which was less than complimentary. I noticed, however, that a pattern emerged when one looked closely at the sources. Often, there existed some degree of rivalry between Altovise and those interviewed. One was left with a one-dimensional vision of her, when it was presented by her adversaries. At first, I wondered how she'd managed to make such formidable enemies, but my research would also provide some insight into this area. As with other celebrities, people in Sammy's inner circle were very territorial and protective of their positions. They constantly competed for power and influence, and Altovise had occasionally bumped heads with some of them.

Following Sammy's death, there were numerous stories that covered the insolvency of his estate, and some were rather bizarre. While most agreed that Altovise was the unfortunate victim in that calamitous season, she made a number of imprudent decisions that created still more turmoil. Some reports suggested that she'd actually removed Sammy's glass eye, while other's claimed she retrieved his jewelry from the casket. During the good years, Altovise would have laughed at the lunacy of such thoughts. The seizure of their belongings for a public auction was unthinkable. However, that's exactly what she'd face, and much worse.

The media had a field day. Although the stories of the fallout were grim, Altovise was portrayed as a, somewhat tainted, damsel in distress. I reasoned that, if unfavorable images of her persisted, it was mostly due to her own lengthy silence.

Altovise, literally, vanished for many years, leaving many to speculate about her whereabouts and fate. Anyone seeking to cover the full story was at a loss, because only Altovise truly knew it. It was she who had navigated through the complicated channels which few, if any, women, had traveled. Having paid heavy dues, she'd earned the right to speak about them. After all, no one else could express the things in her heart, but the woman herself.

When this fact finally hit home, I knew why Altovise's general image didn't reflect the woman that I'd befriended. What I'd witnessed, she couldn't have faked. Altovise loved being with people, especially children. She cared very deeply about kids, and dreamed of writing delightful stories to entertain them. This particular trait didn't start late in life. For many years she'd worked for philanthropic organizations and performed each year for SHARE, Inc., a nonprofit group that raised money for developmentally disabled and neglected children. She loved this type of work and spoke of it often.

The dilemma kept me up at night, because I wasn't sure how to address all the issues we'd have to handle. Even after all these years, friends and relatives would still ask, cynically, "Isn't she broke?"

Like countless others, their last image of Sammy's estate was one of financial ruin. I always shrugged, for, I was never certain of how to respond. It was difficult to assess Altovise's situation, but I felt very badly for her. I'd had my own share of financial problems, but couldn't begin to imagine the magnitude of hers. Much of the debt had been reduced, but I wasn't sure of how much she still owed.

I agonized over this for some time and then reached a conclusion. Altovise needed to clear her name. I felt that she'd suffered long enough. It was not only time for her to build a new life, but to speak out about her old one. So, during one of the following meetings with her, I had a heart-to-heart discussion about this.

"Altovise," I began "This is your opportunity to speak up for yourself. Let people know who you really are."

She smiled in agreement, but still, we made little progress.

I began to worry about another possible obstacle. Altovise, Lisa, and Tracey openly joked about me having a Pollyanna-like image, but I knew that I was no angel. Like everyone else, I'd made mistakes and was destined to make many more. So, on various occasions, I shared with Altovise some of the unpleasant episodes in my life – experiences that I wasn't proud of – like when I'd experimented with marijuana in college. I assumed that, since I'd opened up in this manner, she'd feel more comfortable about doing the same. After all, there was great value in what she'd learned. Altovise could teach and forewarn youths about the dangers of indulging in harmful substances. Her past would be a vivid example of a long battle, not only with substance abuse, but other things that had once enslaved her. No one would criticize her, especially after reforming her life.

Altovise, however, would only listen for a while, and make a few vague references to a family member who'd once smoked marijuana. I realized that she still wasn't ready to go back and face her past.

Deep inside, I began to sense that something else had caused the block, a problem that I'd initially overlooked. Perhaps, Altovise's marriage had been more tragic than controversial. When she accepted Sammy's world and all that came with it, she'd paid a steep price for the entrance ticket. Considering the enormity of the sexual and emotional demands that she'd accepted, Altovise may have suffered her greatest heartache long before Sammy's death. For the sake of their union, she'd sacrificed a great deal of herself, gambling with fate like a high-stakes poker player.

Sammy, himself, had spoken about this once in a T.V. interview, and later recorded in his book. With sincere regrets, he mentioned that he'd taken a good woman who'd come from a good family and introduced her to the darkest side of life. It had destroyed her.

Suddenly, a frightening question occurred to me. What happens when you've sold your soul, and then, everything that you've bought suddenly collapses?

It seemed to me that it reflected the ultimate state of bankruptcy.

I wasn't a psychoanalyst, but I believed that Altovise needed to get back in touch with herself, the woman she was before marrying Sammy. Once she established her own vision and goals, she could finally have her own life. Then, with a list of new accomplishments, she'd have a greater sense of self-worth. I felt certain that, once she experienced some degree of success, she'd begin to heal. I had confidence that Altovise could do this. She just needed a little jump-start.

Altovise and I were eating dinner one night, when we began to brainstorm about a story we'd write. We both wanted to convey a powerful message to children and teens, and it seemed like the best way to reach them.

Altovise reminded me that Sammy wanted her to urge young people, especially artists, to stay in school and strive for excellence. I'd embraced a similar feeling, having had a mother who was a strong teacher and advocate for education.

There was another important message that I longed to deliver.

"Our young girls" I began, "They're growing up with degrading images. If we don't create positive ones for them, how will they develop healthy self-images?"

At this point, I got a bit carried away, and my words were probably bordering on preaching, but I had to speak from my heart. I was pained by what I often saw. The heavy emphasis on violence and all the "bump and grind" images of young women made me sick. There was a real drought, when it came to quality films, particularly for minorities.

"Where are the wholesome stories and positive role models for our kids?" I asked. And what ever happened to love?" I asked.

"There aren't enough fairy tales for our young children," I complained. "Or romantic stories for girls."

Altovise looked at me oddly, then slowly nodded.

I felt that, together, we could make a difference. We could create beautiful stories that would inspire kids to be better people and ultimately change their lives. "Our children need more than what they've been given. They need uplifting messages," I stressed.

I wanted to offer inspiration to youth, and encourage them to strive for their dreams, even when they were hit by adversity. I didn't have all the answers, and didn't even have a good story idea, but the spiritual part of me knew that God was love, and people needed love, above all else.

We both thought about it, and agreed that the best way to deliver a powerful story was in an attractive package. "We'll dazzle them," Altovise said, which was also my desire, and I chuckled, "With a spoonful of sugar!"

What could be more ideal, than to use entertainment? Hadn't Sammy spent most of his life entertaining the public? Why not employ the same medium to get his message across to kids? We decided to try our hand at writing a screenplay, to actually create a musical film.

The more we thought about it, the more we liked it, especially as a way to reach out to young artists. There was no questioning the fact that film and television made a huge impact on kids. We knew, all too well, about the negative influences. Now, we'd use the same medium to deliver uplifting images.

It wasn't as though we were dabbling in foreign waters. Altovise had appeared in a few movies and T.V. shows, and I'd written a proposal for a children's T.V. program, and two scripts for the sample episodes. As far as I knew, however, the producers still hadn't sold it. At least, they'd never mailed the $6,000 they still owed me.

Of course, it may have had something to do with my refusal to write anything promoting the occult. I'd agreed to create the show, but only if I could build it around angels instead of the occult theme they initially had in mind. Not surprisingly, they thought I was crazy, which made my stand a bit more challenging, especially since I wasn't in a comfortable position. I was a single mom battling with arthritis – following nine hip surgeries – and the financial problems that had resulted. Despite this, I couldn't promote what I knew was wrong.

I explained that young people were bombarded with dark and destructive messages, especially sexually explicit and violent imagery, and I couldn't promote anything else that was harmful. In fact, my dream was to teach kids about God's love and his wonderful miracles. So, I incorporated an angelic theme into screenplay, and when it was completed, sent it to the producers. Well, the check never came.

Looking back, I'd learned an unforgettable lesson about the pitfalls of working without a signed contract, and also gained a valuable gift. I had acquired the skills and experience needed to write great screenplays. Perhaps, now, it would be worth the ordeal.

I began to believe that it was part of my destiny to work with Altovise. After all, we were on similar missions: I wanted to promote higher values, and she wanted to promote higher education. I wasn't sure of how we'd combine the two, but believed that if I prayed hard enough, the story would come together.

Like a cheerleader, I chanted: "We can do this! We can do this!"

"Yeah!" replied Altovise, beaming. "We can do this!"

# 5

## A DETOUR TO MEXICO

*Late March – Early April 2005*
*Sarasota, Florida*

"Was there really an Orient Express?" I asked Altovise. We were riding in the car, considering different story ideas, when I had a vision of a talented family and their singing group. I thought it would be thrilling to write a mystery aboard a train in Europe. It seemed to me that I'd read about the train, but couldn't recall if it still, if ever, existed. Before she could answer, another thought came to mind, and we started discussing another scenario.

Altovise had traveled extensively. She'd seen exotic places and met some of the world's most extraordinary people, and she had a wealth of experiences from which to draw. We realized that, through our stories, we could take kids on fascinating journeys, introduce them to historic sites and characters, and retrace significant passages in history.

First, we agreed that our travelers would compete in a talent competition in Europe. Then, a few days later, we decided to use a location closer to home – Mexico. It occurred to me that Mexico was an increasingly important neighbor. Although many of its citizens traveled to the United States, there was still a huge void in our knowledge of Mexican culture and history. Appreciation of their language was also important.

"Alto, our kids need to know and speak Spanish in order to compete in the future."

Altovise agreed, so we decided to incorporate as much Spanish as we could into the dialogue.

Over the following days, our story seemed to bud like a flower. Our fictitious family would have an unforgettable adventure from which they'd gain new insights about life. We'd entertain kids – dazzling them a bit – and in the process, dramatize the importance of education. We'd open up a whole new world and invite kids to come out and explore it.

Since we'd both spent considerable time in Mexico, we began to share memories of our trips. Altovise described the coastal scenery of Acapulco and how much she'd enjoyed water skiing there. I offered anecdotes about Oaxaca and the narrow roads I took through the mountains to get there.

At Barnes & Noble, we headed to the travel section and began researching various details about the country. Altovise was good at selecting tourist books and found some of the most intriguing bits of information we'd use. In one guide, she found a fascinating picture of a celestial-looking light, and it conjured such a vivid memory of the show, *Star Trek*, that I laughed, "Beam me up, Scotty." Mesmerized, we both gazed at the picture. In a powerful beam that was as focused as stage lighting, the sun's rays poured down into the opening of a cave at Xochicalco, an archaeological site in Mexico; this awe-inspiring occurrence took place only twice a year.

"Wow," I exclaimed. It felt like we'd struck oil. Immediately, we decided that the family – now called the Langstons – would be en route to Acapulco, just in time to experience this event.

That night, I discovered that Altovise had a special eye for magical elements. She had this uncanny way of spotting charming nuggets of information that might have otherwise been overlooked. A few minutes later she brought, yet, another treasure.

Chuckling with delight, Altovise read a passage in a book about a folkloric myth that intrigued her. "It's believed," she said, "that a wolf-monster prowls around some of Mexico's most mountainous regions."

"Great!" I said, captivated by the tale. "We can have our travelers take that route." We decided that our family wouldn't confront or actually engage the monster. We'd just use the legend to spice up the atmosphere.

I paused a moment, marveling at how fast Altovise had found these things. Actually, I was taken aback, because, initially, she'd seemed more interested in gazing at a book about Frank Sinatra. Then, she appeared to be browsing through the aisles in a day-dreamy sort of way. I'd learn, however, that it was just her way. When you least expected it, Altovise always surprised you.

We studied maps of Arizona and Mexico and compared various routes for the trip. I'd later use the Internet to help us determine the most realistic time frames and the distances between locations.

We'd return to Barnes & Noble a few days later. By then, we'd staked out our route, created the main characters, and outlined most of the plot. We considered different modes of transportation, more maps and timeframes, and multiple scenarios.

Finally, we decided that the Langstons would travel by way of a large, comfortable RV. This would give them the opportunity to explore the back roads of 'the real Mexico,' rather than just arrive at a popular tourist attraction. They'd meet people, see historic places, and gain a broader perspective of the Mexico culture.

Early on, it was obvious that Altovise and I had distinctly different views, when it came to our characters. I was raising a daughter and Altovise had raised a son, and these experiences influenced how we envisioned the Langstons. Sometimes, we disagreed on the type of personalities they had. So we made a quick decision. Altovise would develop the male roles and I'd handle the girls.

Although I structured the general plot, much of my focus was initially given to creating the teenage girl, Kimberly (or Kim). I spent hours imagining the way she thought and behaved, and the importance of her role.

Altovise was much more involved in the development of Kim's brothers, particularly the adolescent we'd named Nathan. I knew that she was thinking of Manny, even before she mentioned it, because she had a special glow in her eyes when she described him.

I insisted on helping create Alex's character, the older, antagonistic brother who threatens to sabotage the group's performance with his own brand of mutiny.

Admittedly, I thought of my daughter, Sandra, when I envisioned the youngest of the Langstons, adorable little Abby.

A true romantic, I hoped to recreate the magical aura that I'd once witnessed on television. That evening, Beyonce` was performing in a stunning evening gown that conveyed the image of a princess. Just before ending the song, she gracefully extended her hand, just as a white dove flew across the stage and landed on it. The scene was stunning and I wanted the same type of enchantment for our story.

I had the perfect partner, because when it came to story-telling, Altovise had an outstanding gift. She was light years ahead of me when she suggested a major twist in the plot that I initially didn't get. It involved a special character whom we'd spent a considerable amount of time trying to shape. He was born rather unexpectedly, while we were having tea in the coffee shop.

That night, we'd had a long conversation about Mexican cities and I recalled the ancient temples and pyramids I'd visited, as well as the open markets and quaint, colorful inns. Some of my fondest memories were of the Zocolo, the open square which served as the center of activity in downtown Oaxaca. Filled with vibrant music and entertainers, busy restaurants and bustling crowds, it was the best place to sit and people-watch. Local Oaxacans and tourists, alike, would flock to the area to enjoy the festive atmosphere.

It was there, while eating lunch, that children would pull up seats and ask permission to eat my leftovers. Waiters tried to shoo them away, but I always gave them money for food, small trinkets, and when a carnival was visiting, some coins for rides and souvenirs. They'd gather at my table like it was a convention center, and in their broken

English, make efforts to talk with me. My most vivid memories were of the most talented children who often played their harmonicas, accordions, and guitars.

Altovise nodded as she listened and began to consider such a scene in our story. I envisioned an adorable young Mexican boy with big expressive eyes, who, for some reason, attached himself to the Langstons. I was drawing from memories of one youth, in particular, whom I'd met on my last visit to Oaxaca. He was no older than ten, but his music, maturity, and knowledge of life, seemed far beyond his age. He often played his guitar for tourists and seemed to make quite a business for himself. Like most people, I was stunned by the romanticized manner in which he played, because his music was so passionate that it ignited a warm flame within me. Had my eyes been closed, I would have sworn that a man – a worldly, older man – was performing. I'd never forget the music he played, and I'd always wonder, where the knowledge of love came from at such a young age.

My last memory of the boy was just as strong. It was late one night when I saw him hail a cab, apparently retiring from a long day of work. As I crossed the street, I wondered if his parents were home, worried about his whereabouts, and when he'd return. The cab disappeared down the street, and as I walked toward my lodging, I continued to think of the boy. What an amazing life he led.

Altovise and I agreed that we wanted this boy in our story. We gave him the name Miguel Z. Alvarez. After tossing around different ideas for his role, we decided that Miguel's presence would impact the outcome of the story. Since we were writing a musical, the boy's music would serve a specific purpose, one which conveyed a powerful message about love. Like an angel, he'd be an almost omnipresent character, eventually changing the lives of all the other characters.

"He'll save the day for the Langstons," I said. "And bring the family back together, or something."

We weren't sure of how it played out, only that Miguel provided the link that tied the whole plot together. There were many messages we wanted to convey, but for me, the most important was the value of love.

Oddly enough, when Altovise came up with the most crucial piece, I thought it was absolutely crazy. She thought Miguel should travel with the family to Acapulco, but, for a while, in total secrecy.

"What if Miguel hides away in their RV?" said Altovise, her eyes bright with excitement. "And nobody knows, of course. But when they leave town, he goes with them."

"Huh?" I responded, somewhat dumbfounded. "Well..." I stuttered, unable to process it. I didn't want to dampen her enthusiasm, but the idea really seemed over-the-top.

"Well, that's a thought," I finally muttered.

During the night, however, the idea came back to me, and by morning, I knew it was brilliant. I couldn't wait to call Altovise and tell her so. At that point, I knew we'd embarked on something special.

# 6

## ADVENTURES AT SEA

*April 6, 2005*
*Sarasota, Florida*

"Oh, my goodness!" cried Altovise, looking grief-stricken. I was driving to the grocery store and had just turned on the radio when we heard the latest news broadcast. Prince Rainier of Monaco had died.

"Oh, goodness," she sighed, again.

"You knew him?" I asked, already sensing the answer. She'd known nearly every celebrity I'd inquired about.

"Oh, yes," she replied. "The whole family. I'm really sorry to hear that."

Wow! I thought. She knew the royal family. I could barely contain my curiosity, especially about Princess Grace. I'd seen her in Alfred Hitchcock's classic **Rear Window**, and although I thought she was a great actress, I was much more intrigued by her later life in Monaco. After all, what woman didn't wonder what it's like to marry a prince? Before I could utter the first question, however, Altovise spoke of an incident which occurred there.

"Several years ago," she said. "Sammy was scheduled to perform in Monaco for a special anniversary celebration. They provided us with a huge yacht to use while we were there. It was actually part of Sammy's payment."

Altovise recalled that on the same day that Sammy was to perform, he learned that he'd been assigned to sit at the head table.

"But, not me!" she stressed, indignantly. "They actually hadn't included me! They completely disrespected me!"

This was the first time I'd ever seen a hint of hurt or anger on Altovise's face. Obviously, she still felt upset over the slight.

"Sammy was furious," she continued. "And he refused to perform!"

"What?" I asked, stunned. "But, they corrected the error, didn't they?"

Altovise shrugged her shoulders. "We left," she said, with a chuckle. "We just sped away in the yacht."

"You're kidding!" I replied.

"No," she replied. "They had to get Bill Cosby and some other performers to take Sammy's place."

Astonishing as it sounded, the story was not only true, but well documented. In fact, from other accounts, I learned that it actually took place in May 1974, while the royal family – along with over 4,000 subjects – was celebrating Prince Rainier's Silver Jubilee. It was the twenty-fifth anniversary of his sovereignty in Monaco. It was actually a two week celebration, and there were 650 guests invited to this particular affair. Differing accounts were written about the episode, and one author suggested that both Sammy and Altovise were snubbed.

In fact, Sammy complained that he hadn't been invited to the same galas as were the white performers. Upon his return to the United States, he reportedly told the press, "The Princess thought I was just another jig in the woodpile."

As I pulled into the parking lot of the grocery store, Altovise mentioned that she'd send a condolence message to the family. I thought that she might find a lovely card inside, and I volunteered to take it to the post office. Altovise, however, felt that a telegram was more appropriate.

"Are you sure you don't prefer a pretty card?" I asked.

"No," she said firmly, her tone indicating that it would be in poor taste.

"Alright," I replied. I wasn't going to argue over a card, as she obviously knew the protocol.

Altovise asked me to compose the message, call the embassy for contact information, and determine the best address to use. A very kind woman at the consulate's office suggested that I send the letter via e-mail. So, a few days later, with Altovise's approval, I did just that.

I remember writing the message on my computer, then pausing for a moment, just prior to sending it. For some reason, I was touched by Altovise's gesture. Maybe it was because, in times of loss, we transcend issues that divide us and reach beyond ourselves in an effort to comfort others. For Altovise, it must have been a solemn time of reflection. Several years had passed and a great deal had transpired since that infamous event. She'd lost Sammy, and now, both the Prince and Princess were gone.

I was pleased to contact the royal family on Altovise's behalf, and I'd always assume that they received her message. Someone certainly opened the email, because, from then on, I'd receive monthly newsletters from the Government of Monaco's Tourist Office.

The imagery conjured by the scenario in Monaco brings to mind another high seas adventure, one which held even greater significance to Altovise.

One day, while I was running errands with her, I asked how she and Sammy actually started dating. Altovise gleefully conveyed the story of their courtship.

It was April 1969, and it began as a Caribbean vacation for four couples. With two yachts awaiting them, the group would spend ten days of sun-filled, carefree sailing, just off of the Bahamas. The famous actor, Sidney Poitier, had dreamed it up. He was sure the excursion would be great for Sammy, who needed a break from his hectic pace. The rest of the party included Poitier's girlfriend, composer Quincy Jones and his wife, and another friend, Terry McNeely and his girlfriend. Sammy was also told to bring a date, and he decided to invite the attractive actress, Peggy Lipton, who was one of the stars from *The Mod Squad*, a popular sitcom during the 1960s. Sammy met Lipton when he starred in a recent episode of the show.

Altovise says that Lipton wasn't getting along with Sammy or the women on the trip, and she abruptly decided to return home. Sammy felt awkward, being left without a companion. So, Poitier's girlfriend, Joanna Shimkus, came up with the idea of inviting Altovise. Sammy appeared to be very fond of her while they worked on the show, *Golden Boy*, and they thought that her presence might cheer him up.

The group delayed their voyage that day, hoping to reach Altovise, who was back in New York. They tried to make contact, but when they hadn't heard back from her by the following morning, they departed, leaving a message for her through Shirley Roades (Sammy's conductor's wife). Sammy also arranged for the reservation of a seaplane to transport Altovise to their yacht. There was no guarantee, but they all hoped that she'd show up.

Late that afternoon, Altovise finally got the message, and took the seaplane to join the group in the Bahamas. Upon arrival, she found a very jubilant welcoming committee, for the crew as well as the vacationers broke into a wild applause.

As Poitier recalled in his memoir, *This Life*, "Sammy Davis Jr., was the happiest person in the fleet. Altovise Gore was a special kind of special. She made the difference, and it showed on Sammy's face."

"We had a fabulous time," said Altovise. "And at the end of that trip, we knew… well, everyone kind of sensed, that something had changed. We weren't the same."

She was right. As they sailed out to sea their friendship crossed into a new channel, and a year later they became Mr. and Mrs. Davis.

A number of books concur with this account of their courtship and offer stories that shed greater light on its inception. The sparks actually began much earlier, during the 1968 London premier of Sammy's show, *Golden Boy*. He was still married to May, but intimately involved with the gorgeous dancer, Lola Falana, who was appearing in his show. During that time, Sammy arranged for Altovise, also performing in the show, to move from her modest lodgings at a boarding house to the more glamorous accommodations which he enjoyed at the Playboy Club. There, Sammy resided in the penthouse suite lent to him by Hugh Hefner, and Lola stayed in a suite two floors below. He convinced Lola to share her dwelling with Altovise, and as history would attest, they'd eventually share a great deal more in common.

Sammy liked being seen with beautiful women, and particularly loved the notoriety of strolling down streets with, both, Lola and Altovise locked on his arms. So, he often took the two leggy and statuesque dancers out on the town. The fun-loving threesome began to hang out fairly regularly, dining in restaurants and visiting clubs, and during that time Altovise and Sammy started flirting with one another. The attraction didn't immediately lead to their involvement, but it was strong enough to capture the attention of several others.

Altovise once mentioned this period to me, but not with regard to their actual courtship. It was during our first conversation, when I'd asked about their children and she'd briefly mentioned her first encounter with one of Sammy's kids. The incident took place in London and specifically involved Sammy's daughter, Tracey. Sammy, who partied heavily, was known to carouse with numerous women. So, his daughter had to compete with several others girls for his time. The seven-year-old was especially hurt by her father's attention to Lola and Altovise. As Altovise recalled, she threw an unforgettable temper tantrum.

"Finally," she said, "Sammy packed her bags and we sent her home."

Thus, began a power struggle between Altovise and her future stepdaughter, a war over Sammy's ever-shifting affections, and a bitter feud that would outlast even her twenty-year marriage.

# 7

## LET'S GO FLY A KITE

*April 2005*
*Sarasota, Florida*

I'd spent so much time working with Altovise that I began to feel like an absentee mother. I knew my daughter missed me and I missed her, too. So, I realized it was time to bring Sandra along. At least, whenever it was possible. I wondered, though, how it would affect our work. Altovise and I needed to stay focused. Sandra was very well behaved, but I worried that she might grow restless. I thought about some of our research projects. Altovise and I had recently visited Campbell's RV dealership. We toured several trailers to consider the best model for our story. We took pictures to help us describe the rooms and plan the scenes. There were still several details to research, like camping facilities and common camping practices, so it was important for us to stay on task. I wondered how to balance everything, with a seven-year-old now in tow. Would it appear unprofessional, or diminish the seriousness of our work? I wondered how Altovise and Sandra would get along.

"Now, don't gawk at her," I'd told Sandra, that first day. "Be nice to her. And don't start asking questions about her husband."

I'd picked up Sandra from school after dropping Altovise off at the market. I was driving back to the store when I looked at Sandra in my rearview mirror. She looked deep in thought, like she was concentrating on her manners. When I arrived at Publix, Altovise was just coming out of the door, so I pulled over to the curb to load up her groceries.

"Alto," I said, "This is my daughter, Sandra."

A smile crept across Altovise's face. "I love your braids," she exclaimed. "They look just like mine when I was your age."

My worries were unfounded. Altovise wasn't the least bit irritated by Sandra's presence. Actually, she enjoyed her. I was amazed by how well she and Sandra hit it off. Within only a few minutes they were laughing hysterically, and Altovise was completely transformed.

Giggling, with a voice much younger than hers, Altovise assumed the character of a little girl. From that day on, she'd always reserve this role just for Sandra, who would always be delighted by it.

I began to realize that Altovise was very young at heart, and it was this giddy, whimsical, part of her personality that helped shape our most endearing characters.

One evening always stands out in my memory. Earlier that day, I'd promised Sandra to take her on a kite-flying outing on Siesta Key Beach. Only, Altovise and I were so busy running errands that it was dark by the time we got there. Undiscouraged, Sandra still wanted to go out on the beach, this, despite a foggy mist that had settled along the coast. I didn't share her enthusiasm for a couple of reasons. First, I'd bought the flimsy kite at a dollar store, and the material looked so cheap I wasn't sure if it was worth the effort. Second, I didn't feel comfortable about being out on the beach so late. It was more than just dark; it was misty.

As it turned out, Altovise hadn't been to any of the Keys and she also wanted to see one of the beaches. She agreed with Sandra that we should go. So, since it was two against one, the three of us forged ahead toward the water.

It was a breezy night and the moving fog created an almost eerie aura. Although my expectations weren't high, the flight of the kite certainly was. Almost immediately, it was swept up into the mist, where it danced and frolicked like a monarch butterfly. Thrilled, Sandra and Altovise jumped and skipped along the sand, and as they took turns guiding the toy, I marveled at how much fun it was. During those enchanting moments, as we danced in the wind, we all seemed like kindred spirits. I'd later recall only two other occasions when I'd felt that type of elation, and they'd occurred many years before. That night, I felt very young and carefree again, and I sensed that Altovise did, too.

We didn't look like the Three Musketeers, but after that, our adventures reminded me of them. Sandra would hang out with us more frequently, and we'd sometimes go to the movies. Altovise and I would watch the credits roll at the end and try to imagine our own names listed up on the screen.

One afternoon, after watching *Racing Stripes*, we just sat and savored the thought.

"One day," I said dreamily, "we'll be up there, too."

I'd tried to imagine our characters coming to life, speaking the words that we'd given them. By now, Kim and Alex were very real, at least in my mind, and I often had to stop and record new things they said. Sometimes, it was late at night and I'd have to make quick notes. However, it was always worthwhile. The characters had become a part of me, and I wondered how I'd feel when real actors portrayed them. Would the audiences respond to them?

Increasingly, I dreamed of the Langston kids and anticipated the day when they'd finally come to life.

Altovise and I smiled when we thought of eventually seeing our film.

"One day, Alto," I said, assuredly. "One day."

# 8

## I NEED A HERO

*April 2005*
*Sarasota, Florida*

In the weeks ahead, I'd marvel at how Altovise and Tracey managed to live together, because I sensed a strange uneasiness building between them. I couldn't quite put my finger on it, but if a physician had tried to describe their condition, he may have diagnosed it as a mild case of tolerance with a fragile state of coexistence. As events unfolded at Medici Court the atmosphere would prove to be unhealthy for more than one reason.

Altovise and Tracey now phoned fairly regularly for rides to the market, to the chiropractor, and to run various errands. Whenever the three of us were in the car, Tracey always directed the conversation toward Altovise. It was awkward, because it was almost as though I wasn't present. What surprised me most, however, were the comments Tracey made when we were alone together.

During those moments, when I was suddenly visible, Tracey revealed the thoughts that were increasingly preoccupying her. She was still very distant, but she'd grown so frustrated with her situation that she began to vent, even to me. Earlier, she'd boasted that she'd been promised a six-figure salary, but those dollars hadn't materialized. In fact, her references to someone named Barrett, and complaints about money, would eventually dominate all of her conversations. I noticed that, the days when she was most upset were those on which she'd argued with Barrett.

Despite this, Tracey was determined to get one thing straight. The first day that we were alone together in the car, she told me, right off the bat, that she was Altovise's assistant and it was part of her job to handle Altovise's correspondence. Furthermore, if anyone should write Altovise's memoir, the best candidate was Burt Boyar.

"He wrote Sammy's books," said Tracey. So, in her opinion, there was no better writer, and certainly not some unknown woman from Sarasota.

I was taken aback by Tracey's bluntness. It was our first real conversation and in less than ten minutes, she'd taken it upon herself to dismiss me from any writing assignments I may have considered. Obviously, I wasn't supposed to get comfortable, thinking there was room for my services, other than driving them around, of course.

I kept driving as though I hadn't heard her.

By then, Altovise and I were focusing solely on our screenplay, so Tracey's words really didn't matter to me. I was initially concerned about the viability of Altovise's autobiography, and therefore, my own role, but I'd already moved toward the direction I sensed was best, at least for the moment. I'd help Altovise build a writing career, and possibly earn some screenplay credits, so she'd have something uplifting to share when it was finally time to write her book. I felt comforted, in knowing that she'd taken steps to overcome her past defeats, and her successful new life would be an inspiration to others.

During that period, however, Lisa began to call much more frequently. I wasn't sure if she was actually sharing or fishing for information, but the things she revealed were very disturbing. There were new, troubling developments in Altovise's life, and they were unfolding on a day-to-day basis. By now, Lisa realized that Altovise wouldn't be opening a dance school in Sarasota. Nor, was it likely that she'd purchase a new home. The problem, she said, was so complicated that she couldn't fully grasp or make sense of it.

Altovise's managers, or partners, exercised enormous power over all of her affairs. Each week, it became more evident that she didn't have a real say in matters concerning, not only her business interests, but much of her personal life.

Still more alarming was the murky and ill-defined boundary line between Altovise's finances and that of her managers. Whatever arrangements were made concerning Altovise's royalty payments, they seemed grossly inadequate, because she was often pinched for cash. According to Tracey, this caused growing tensions, as the partners competed to get the mailed checks each month.

At this point, I began to hear about another man named Tony, who seemed to live somewhere nearby, and I began to understand Tracey's jokes about "racing to the mailbox." Friends suspected that Altovise was being short-changed, and that was only one of their growing fears.

Back then, I wasn't sure of Tracey's exact role, so I didn't put much stock in her interpretation of their situation. If any of her claims were true, though, and the managers were manipulating Altovise, it was still out of my hands. I didn't even know the two men; we hadn't been introduced. I merely wrote the stories, pumped the gas, and drove the car. That was the extent of my involvement. I felt that, it Tracey had a nasty run-in with the managers, she'd have to write that page herself.

I guess, there's no wrath like that of a jaded employee, and when it came to spilling the beans, Tracey made sure that they spilled all over the floor. As their problems escalated, Tracey stopped snickering about the checks in the mailbox, because it was no longer humorous. Her complaints intensified and her list of grievances grew longer. Near the top was the lack of transportation. After several months in Florida, they were still without a car and often had to walk down University Parkway, just to get needed supplies from a drug store.

In one conversation, Tracey mentioned that Tony became indignant when she claimed that he'd gone to a speaking engagement that Altovise was scheduled to attend. She thought he'd actually accepted the speaker's fee. Tracey also said that Tony, who was short and framed much like Sammy, was once wearing one of the entertainer's fur jackets when she spotted him leaving their apartment. Tracey immediately called for Altovise, who emerged from her bedroom and told him to bring it back.

Then, there was a troubling incident that took place while Altovise was visiting her mother in New York. Tony, who was apparently a co-signer on many of Altovise's business documents, had borrowed a cluster of her keys from Tracey. With them, he went to Altovise's bank on University Parkway and opened her safety deposit box, removing the bulk of her valuables. Most of the items taken were jewelry, and although he'd later tell me "They weren't really valuable," he didn't return the goods until he was pressured by one of Altovise's most persuasive friends.

The relations were already strained between Tony, Tracey, and Altovise. This incident, however, ignited a number of heated confrontations, the most dramatic of which occurred when a visiting friend named Josh picked up the phone and called his father. I don't know the exact words that were exchanged, only that when Tony was summoned to the phone, he was speaking with the outraged former head of the Nation of Islam, Minister Louis Farrakhan. The essence of his message was to the point: Tony was to return Altovise's belongings without delay. With that, Tony finally returned her things, but two years later, Altovise would tell me that a few important items were still missing.

Lisa, who was fuming over the incident, called to share the details with me. She seemed irritated that I didn't respond by taking a definite stand. Like Altovise's other friends, she was deeply worried about the situation and couldn't imagine why things were so out of control. Most baffling of all was Altovise's behavior. No one understood why she didn't sever her ties with the two men.

Lisa must have been looking for answers, but since Altovise hadn't provided any, I was in the dark.

"What type of hold do they have on her?" she asked. "It doesn't make any sense! Unless, they have something on her."

Tracey, however, was finished with all the speculation. She began a forceful campaign to discredit and retire Altovise's managers. By then, she'd conducted quite a bit of research, digging up records and articles she'd found on the Internet and rummaging through Altovise's private papers when she was away. What she found gave her the chills. So, she made phone calls to friends and various contacts for more details. New, disturbing facts kept turning up and eventually, Tracey thought she'd pooled together enough evidence to convince Altovise to break all ties with the men.

Looking back, this would be a costly mistake. Like everyone else, Tracey underestimated the extent of the managers' power, and unfortunately, the only one positioned for the ax was Tracey, herself. Another campaign seemed to go into effect, a counterattack that would become extremely vicious.

I began to notice a few subtle changes. Altovise, who'd never openly complained about Tracey, suddenly mentioned that her roommate hadn't helped pay the rent. With only a slight nod, I acknowledged her comment, but since Tracey hadn't been paid, as promised, I wasn't going to go there. That issue was between Altovise and her roommate, so I simply changed the subject.

While shopping a few days later, Altovise grumbled about how annoying it was to keep buying food for her roommate. Again, I made no comment. We'd always brought food and cigarettes back for Tracey, so why was it suddenly a big hassle?

Each day, Altovise's disenchantment with Tracey seemed to grow, as did Tracey's frustration with Altovise. The two women, in fact, were now almost always at odds. I didn't have to wonder why the rift was occurring, or who primarily benefitted from this. I just worried about where they were heading. It couldn't be good.

I was just as mystified by Altovise's relationship with Tracey, as I was about her partners, but I was determined to honor the "See No Evil" rule. At this point, I didn't trust anything, not even my own perceptions, so, I also embraced another idiom, "Ignorance Is Bliss." Although the questions began to taunt me, I'd made up my mind to stay out of the way. Altovise and I were writing partners, and her personal life was none of my business.

To maintain these boundaries, I focused solely on our film project. We'd made some headway in developing the plot, and since the main characters were now born, I wrote the first drafts of the opening scenes. Over dinner, Altovise and I discussed two new characters, just as though we were oblivious to the chaos unfolding.

As the war waged on between Tracey, Altovise and her partners, I edited the script and restructured the outline. Between the troubling calls that came from Lisa, I worked to strengthen and fine-tune the dialogue. When Lisa phoned, warning me of an impending crisis, I typed the revisions of all the first scenes.

Even as stress and fatigue began to set in, I found new ways to keep the characters moving. I kept writing, even as Lisa shared her concerns about Tracey's health. I wasn't blind. I knew the situation was deteriorating, yet, I focused entirely on our plot, at least, for the moment. I believed, that if there was any help I could offer, it was tied to the work. Nothing could be accomplished from a position of weakness. To make a real difference, I had to keep my hands on the keyboard. So, I forced myself to keep typing. I didn't really know all the details, but one thing was clear: Altovise was powerless to change anything, at least, from her current position. In order to change this, and give her some leverage, I'd have to complete and sell our project.

"Focus," I whispered. "You have to stay focused."

There were days when I felt overwhelmed with worries, but refused to get involved in this part of Altovise's life. When she was ready to talk, I'd be there to listen, but I was seeing the same pattern I'd noticed when it came to her past. She may have complained about Tracey, but she hadn't mentioned one word about Barrett or Tony. Once, again, she was only prepared to discuss the "safe" topics.

At times it seemed surreal, the strange way in which we communicated, or failed to. We'd meet almost daily, but delicately dance around the most pressing issues of her life. Driving through town, enjoying the beauty of the scenery, it was like a silent elephant was sitting between us. Altovise smiled pleasantly, as though all was going well, but I always wondered how long she'd keep up the charade. The situation was reaching the breaking point.

As the days passed, I realized that Altovise lived two separate lives. There was the whimsical, childlike fantasy world in which we created wonderful characters. Then, there was the reality that she returned to when she reentered her apartment.

Looking back, she seemed to protect, or isolate, the make-believe world from the one that she couldn't control. Was she afraid to merge the two?

It dawned on me that, with the exception of our initial meetings, Altovise and I rarely spoke of any adult issues. We didn't even discuss Sammy that much, or anyone else over eighteen. Once we discovered our mutual love for children's stories, we drifted into a lifestyle in which, like two big kids, we'd rush off to explore bookstores and libraries, and discuss all the things that kids normally think of.

Perhaps, our work provided Altovise with her only escape from her reality, other than alcohol. On the surface, her life appeared fairly tidy. Back then, there was also no discussion of alcohol or anything else with which she was struggling. Despite this, I was learning a great deal about them. Not from Altovise, with whom I now spent countless hours, but from Lisa and Tracey.

I learned that a few years before, Altovise had entered into a partnership with Barrett LaRoda and Anthony Francis to establish the Sammy Davis, Jr. Foundation, and later, Sammy Davis, Jr. Enterprises. To consummate the deal, she transferred ownership of the Estate of Sammy Davis Jr. to the enterprise, and signed over her rights to Sammy's work, including her share of the intellectual property rights to the books he'd co-authored with Burt Boyar and his wife. For their part, Barrett and Anthony were supposed to promote the entertainer's image and cultivate new business ventures. Barrett and Anthony (called Tony) were entrusted to manage the financial affairs of the organizations, and to manage the Sammy Davis, Jr. Estate. In their agreement, Altovise, Barrett, and Tony were supposed to each earn a one-third share of the group's profits.

Tony, who'd recently purchased a new home, lived in the neighboring town of Bradenton, Florida. Most of the official business was actually performed by his nephew, Barrett, who was based in Reseda, California. His company, The LaRoda Group advised visitors to their Web site that they owned one third of Sammy Davis, Jr. Enterprises, and that they were the exclusive licensor of the Sammy Davis Jr. image and likeness.

It would be two years later, after a heated fight with Tony, when Altovise would reveal another part of their agreement. She didn't actually net one-third share of the profit, at least, not after she finished paying her partners. She said that Barrett charged her a twenty percent commission on all of her income, and she paid an additional ten percent to Tony, "For introducing me to Barrett." Their routine required that she take the checks she received to the bank, where she'd cash them and then pay her partners their commissions. This represented a reversal of the practices of most agents, and meant that Altovise was taxed for the full amount of these payments. The combined commissions exceeded the standard range of ten to fifteen percent which was required by some of the most respected literary and entertainment agencies.

At the same time, there were plans on the table for a film about Sammy's life, as well as a documentary that Altovise would produce with Burt Boyar. Altovise also mentioned an online casino in Sammy's name, and various other ventures they'd discussed. With their hands in virtually all of these pots, the managers were well-positioned for a Sammy Davis Jr. bonanza.

That season, Altovise wasn't ready to question any of their arrangements. She appeared to have put all her faith in her partners, this without closely examining their business practices or credentials. There was only one person who'd started an informal investigation into their partnership – her roommate.

Lisa grew impatient with my position of neutrality. She thought I was living in denial and she was determined to brief me on everything that happened. Perhaps, it was easier to close my eyes than to acknowledge such an ugly situation, especially sense I felt powerless to change it.

One day, when Lisa was pressuring me to take some action, I flipped the question and inquired, "If Alto isn't listening to other friends, what makes you think she'll listen to me?"

Still, I held on to some semblance of hope. My spiritual beliefs assured me that when you reached out to help others, God would be there for you. While I couldn't force my views on anyone, some beliefs were universally accepted. I knew, for example, that one's feelings of self-worth were also influenced by one's accomplishments. When someone achieved success at a given task, or career, it bolstered their confidence and dignity. It was self-affirming and empowering. Without this, one could fake it for a while, but not very long.

I didn't have all the answers, but knew that one of the keys to success was to do what you loved. Altovise loved kids and wanted to create children's stories. Once her stories were published, or she had a film credit under her belt, she'd have a viable new career. She'd be a recognized name in the areas of children's entertainment and literature. Wouldn't this give her something to be proud of, and a greater sense of self-esteem? Wouldn't this be a better high than another shot of vodka?

Perhaps, I'd always been a dreamer. Maybe that's what I shared most in common with Altovise. Still, I'd taken practical steps to give her the leverage needed to put her foot down. Once she had some degree of independence, she could take more control of her life.

I was moving as fast as I could. I'd prepared the materials to apply for the copyright and filed the application in both of our names. I remembered that day, because I was missing only one thing: the name of our screenplay. I called Altovise, and we tossed around a few ideas, when she suddenly shouted out, "A Detour to Mexico!" There was no question about it, the name had the right ring, so we kept it, and I finished the application. I also registered our material with the Writer's

Guild of America. Like a protective mother, I took every precaution to protect it, or, at least, I thought I had.

Days before, I'd questioned Altovise about an important issue. I needed some clarification on the nature of her relationship with her managers. Most importantly, I wanted assurance that our project was legally separate from the Sammy Davis Jr. Estate and that, in the event that we received a contract on our screenplay, Altovise could sign it, herself.

"Your managers don't have to be involved, do they?" I asked, carefully.

"Oh, no," she replied, smiling. "This is separate from them."

"Good," I responded. "So, your managers don't need to know about this right now."

I knew that greed made people do outrageous things, but I'd never witnessed it so closely.

"I just want to make sure the money goes directly to you," I stressed.

Altovise smiled, knowingly, and nodded. I smiled, too, with a deep sigh of relief. It may have seemed like a trivial point, but I knew enough to be cautious. Barrett and Tony operated with the type of heavy-handedness that came only from having carte blanche authority. Thankfully, I wouldn't have to negotiate with the two men, especially since one of them seemed to have enormous influence over her. Although, I was clueless about why this bond existed, I wasn't naive enough to think I could challenge it. Everyone who knew of their partnership was leery of it, but if Altovise regarded these men as heroes, she'd be offended by any allegation made against them. So, no matter how they may have appeared, I'd keep my opinions to myself. This was no time to trespass on what may have been sacred ground.

# 9

## SHE AIN'T MY SISTER

*April 2005*
*Sarasota, Florida*

I would have had only vague memories of Tracey, were it not for two specific developments. In early April, an elderly friend was hospitalized. She required around-the-clock care when she returned home, so Lisa and I tried to arrange and organize the coverage she needed. Since Tracey was a nurse, and desperately needed money, we quickly brought her to help.

A Wall Street pioneer, Edna Rafael had proudly announced she was one of the first women to break into the stock brokerage industry. She seemed equally as proud of another distinctive mantle, that of being an extremely successful matchmaker. Edna didn't hesitate to tell people, even strangers shopping in stores, that she'd brought together thirteen couples. With only one exception, every marriage she'd brokered had withstood the test of time.

"Let me find you a husband," she'd tell me, her eyes sparkling as she considered the candidates.

"No way!" I'd protest. "I'm married to my ministry."

"Such a pretty woman," she'd sigh, with a look that said, "such a waste."

Then, we'd both laugh at one another.

During those moments Edna could be extremely charming, but she was a shrewd woman in every measure. I'd learned this early in our friendship and was quickly reminded on the day we brought Tracey. Edna was immediately leery of her and, during the first week, peered at her closely.

Within only a few days, Edna complained about Tracey's imprudent use of time. I knew that Tracey's tastes in T.V. programs, especially soap operas and sitcoms, didn't measure up to Edna's tough standards. Like a hawk, she still monitored all the financial news updates broadcasted throughout the day. I sometimes ran errands for Edna and took her shopping, so I knew quite a bit about her tastes. She was picky when it came to selecting apples and oranges and was even more finicky when it came to judging people. Therefore, I didn't take her complaints too seriously.

Then, she voiced a new list of concerns. From Edna's observations, Tracey scratched herself entirely too much, and in her opinion, the girl's complexion looked unhealthy. Even at Edna's advanced age, she had spotted something to which I was clueless – the signs of heavy drug use. Since Edna was particular about people, and infamously demanding, she continued to look for reasons to dismiss Tracey. By the third week, she spotted something serious enough to warrant close attention. Increasingly, Tracey spent her hours just stretched across the couch.

"The girl's sick," declared Edna. "I like her, but..." she paused, dramatically. "I feel like I should be caring for her."

Then, a few days later, Tracey called with an urgent request. Altovise was away and she needed something for excruciating pain and wanted me to come and get her. I grabbed Sandra and we rushed to the car. When Tracey gave me the directions, though, I realized we were driving toward the wrong area. In fact, we were headed straight toward a troubled neighborhood, wrought with drug dealing and crime. I was furious with Tracey, but I dropped her off where she'd requested.

Later, I told Lisa I'd never take her for a run like that again, especially with Sandra in the car.

"What on earth is going on?" I asked.

Lisa decided it was time to disclose some things that I didn't know. She said that Tracey and Altovise befriended one another while both were staying at a drug and alcohol rehabilitation facility in Oklahoma. Altovise was recovering from an alcohol binge, while Tracey was trying to harness an addiction to cocaine. In the fall, when Altovise was released, her partners arranged for Tracey to travel and accompany her as an 'assistant.' In reality, Tracey's primary duty was to watch over Altovise, and ensure that she stay sober.

It wasn't serendipity that brought the two women to Sarasota, but Tony Francis, who had also once lived at the Tuscany with his wife.

Things seemed to be getting out of hand and the whole situation was now preoccupying my thoughts. I didn't know what to do. Still, I felt compelled to do something. As a friend of Altovise's, I was feeling uncomfortable about remaining silent. I should have been more supportive and, at least, expressed more about my faith. It was the one thing I felt sure about, and it was what I depended upon for strength. What more could I offer than that?

I recalled one of our first discussions about this, as it was a very memorable evening. Altovise and I were meeting at the Atlanta Bread Company. I'd finished the outline of our story, the treatment, and the latest revisions of our scenes. As Altovise drank her tea, I slowly read over the material.

When I finished, there was something else on my mind. Altovise's calm exterior suggested nothing to reveal it, but there was a great deal of turmoil in her life. I didn't want to be dragged into all the inner fighting, but I could no longer stand by without saying something, so I put the work aside for a moment.

I decided to ease into the conversation by explaining how we'd taken a wonderful step, by reaching out to help others, especially children. I believed that one day we'd be blessed for it.

"It may take a little longer," I admitted, "but it's the right way to do it."

We'd touched on this before, especially since I'd included a spiritual theme in our story. It was subtle, but it was definitely there. I felt obligated to explain my motives and assure Altovise that I wouldn't be preachy. She was comfortable with it, just as long as the message didn't go overboard.

"God won't forget us," I told her, and asked if I could say a short prayer.

I'd seen miracles before and wanted Altovise to know that they still occurred. I knew she desperately needed one, just as I did, so I paused at this point.

I watched her closely for a reaction.

Altovise looked a bit awkward, and then slowly began to speak. She told me that, while she could relate to all these things, in her circles, my views weren't popular. As she searched for the perfect words, I realized she was trying to be diplomatic. In essence, if it got around that she was espousing religious views, it wouldn't go over very well. Friends would probably think she was weird or that she'd gone crazy. Altovise said that she was a Christian and believed in God, but didn't want to appear overly religious, like some zealot, or something.

I understood and knew it was time to move on. I'd planted the seed, though, if she ever wanted to come back to the subject. This gave me some degree of peace. I'd finally said what was in my heart.

# 10

## HEADING TO HOLLYWOOD?

*April 2005*
*Sarasota, Florida*

I thought it was time to get some professional feedback on our work.

I phoned an old friend, Michael Carrington, whom I also considered my mentor. He'd worked in Hollywood for several years, and his numerous writing credits included various episodes of *The Simpsons, The Jamie Foxx Show,* and material for the comedian/actor, Sinbad. He'd also hosted the Nickelodeon children's game show, *Think Fast!* In recent years, he'd written programs specifically geared to the "tween" market, and at the time, Michael was one of the writers and producers of the Disney Channel's hit show, *That's So Raven.*

Michael was extremely talented, high-spirited, and a genius when it came to comedy. With his clean-cut, family-oriented values, he'd found the perfect home in the Disney family. I recommended him to Altovise, knowing that he could critique our work, give sound advice, and hopefully tell us who to talk to.

"Michael's someone we can trust," I said, since I'd known him most of my life. As a boy, he seemed like the archetypal whiz kid. He came from a strong family background and wholesome stock, and his straight-laced appearance attested to it. Our fathers had befriended one another while they attended Talladega College – a historically black college in Alabama – and our families had always been close.

The Carringtons lived in New York, only about fifty minutes from Bridgeport, Connecticut, where I grew up. We often celebrated holidays and other special occasions together. In fact, during a New Year's Eve party at my home, Michael's mom, who was a nurse and midwife, rescued the youngest son of famous Globetrotter, Meadowlark Lemon, when the boy began to choke on a coin he'd swallowed.

I was proud of Michael's accomplishments, and still remembered his first days in television, when he wrote for *The Robert Klein Show.* We went to the taping of the last episode, which was pretty exciting, and it was one of the last two times we'd all gathered in New York. The other occasion was for the New York reception for Michael and his wife, Lynn, following their marriage in Las Vegas. In recent years, I'd always looked forward to opening their Christmas cards, as they traditionally tucked the latest photos of their kids inside.

I felt fortunate to have a stalwart figure like Michael in our corner. I could depend upon him like a brother, and this type of trust factor was crucial, especially in our circumstances. People were already sharing frightening tales of stories being stolen in Hollywood, so it was important to have a good contact on our side.

Looking back, it's odd how things turned out. Michael, and my brother, Todd, had always been drawn to the entertainment field. When I was young, I was more intrigued with politics and foreign affairs. Later, as a journalist working at ABC News, the only dramas that really caught my attention were the clashes that erupted on Capitol Hill. Since I wanted to write and produce documentaries, I'd never seriously considered screenplays, so when the opportunity first presented itself, I was taken aback. This type of format was completely new to me, and I wondered if I'd master it.

When I first called Michael with questions about screenwriting, I was still carrying a lot of insecurity. I wasn't sure that I could make the transition from journalism to entertainment. Michael, however, never had any doubts, at least, none that he expressed. If I was concerned about him taking me seriously, it was unfounded, for he extended a warm welcome mat to the industry, and a great deal of moral support and assistance. Before long, he forwarded some homework for me to study: the scripts from the shows, **That's So Raven** and **Lizzie McGuire.** He also sent the screenwriting software, Final Draft. I felt indebted to him for, despite his demanding schedule, he'd taken the time to help me get started. There's no doubt in my mind that it was Michael's encouragement that gave me the confidence to take my writing seriously. After all, he was working for one of the country's most popular shows. If he thought that I had a chance, I'd give it a try.

During the last week of April, I prepared a package of our material for Michael. I slipped a handwritten note inside, and mailed it to him. His feedback would be invaluable, because we were writing for the same demanding audience. With two children of his own and a host of kids' shows under his belt, who would know better than Michael? He'd let me know if we were on the right track.

The second person I approached was the actor, Geoffrey Owens, who'd played Elvin Tibideaux in **The Cosby Show**. If it seemed coincidental that he shared this **Cosby** experience with **That's So Raven** star, Raven Symone, it seemed just as ironic that he lived at The Tuscany, where Altovise was residing.

Our first meeting didn't actually take place at their apartment complex. I'd initially bumped into him in the parking lot of the Asolo Theater. Geoffrey was teaching a drama class in the back of the building, which was also home to the Sarasota School of Ballet, where my daughter attended. We'd spoken once or twice, but it wasn't until I saw him featured on the nightly news that I decided to contact him. He visited one of the local high schools to talk with at-risk students about the importance of education. That's when a light flashed in my head. If Geoffrey had the same concerns about young people, perhaps he'd be interested in our project.

Michael Carrington called me after reading our material. I held my breath for a moment. After all, this was the first time we'd get an opinion of our work. Did he understand our message? Did he see what we were trying to accomplish? My heart was thumping wildly, and when he finally spoke, it nearly stopped. Michael sounded as excited as I was about the project. He thought we had an impressive story. In fact, he thought it was perfect for Disney Pictures, and suggested that I pitch it to the company.

Michael told me that Denise Carlson was the contact who acquired such materials, but first, he wanted to make some calls. He'd later suggest that we get an agent to represent us and recommended his own, Art Rutter, who was then with Shapiro-Lichtman Talent Agency in Beverly Hills.

Since Altovise had mentioned that she needed to travel to Los Angeles, I suggested that they get together. Michael sounded thrilled by the opportunity, and said he looked forward to hearing from her.

# 11

## THE COSBY CONNECTION

*Early May 2005*
*Sarasota, Florida*

Altovise was summoned to Los Angeles for contract talks, or, at least, that's what she believed. I sensed, however, that something else was developing.

Some may call it intuition, but something warned me that our season together was coming to a close. The trip only confirmed it. Too many things had gone wrong in Sarasota, and the situation at Medici Court had gotten out of control. Actually, it was Tracey who couldn't be controlled. She'd pried around and uncovered too many things, and provoked too many nasty arguments. To Altovise's partners, she'd become much like a prickly thorn, one which was deeply lodged into Altovise's life, and the situation was getting sticky. While, I hoped that I was wrong, something told me that, if they couldn't get rid of the troublesome roommate, then Altovise, like the Queen on a chessboard, would be swiftly moved to a safer place.

There were a number of clues that hinted to this. That's why, when Altovise boarded her plane for L.A., I knew she wasn't coming back, at least, no time soon. Sadly enough, Altovise actually believed that she'd return, but nothing turned out quite as she'd envisioned.

Initially, Altovise was very enthusiastic, as the trip seemed to hold so much promise. She now spoke at length about co-authoring a coffee table book with Burt Boyar. It would feature pictures that Sammy had taken of famous celebrities. Altovise said her husband had been an avid photographer and she was gathering numerous photos that he'd shot. She didn't speak as much about the documentary, only the prospect of this new book.

She and Burt were also considering another joint project, an audio version of one of Sammy's autobiographies.

"This time it will be the actual tapes of Sammy's voice," she said, adding that the only snag was the question of who legally owned Sammy's voice. Was it Burt Boyar, who was Sammy's co-writer, or Altovise, his widow? Altovise felt certain that they'd resolve it amicably.

There were also ongoing discussions about a biopic about Sammy's life. Naturally, this sounded thrilling and Altovise assumed that, with all these lucrative deals in the works, her days of struggling would finally be over. However, that wasn't exactly in the cards, because she wasn't the one who was dealing them.

No matter what developed from the trip, I was committed to completing our work. The prospects for our screenplay also seemed to be promising. Geoffrey, who'd read our initial materials, loved the story. As it turned out, he'd spent considerable time in Oaxaca as a youth. He remembered the setting well, especially the Zocolo, where some of the most important scenes took place. Like myself, he had a special affinity for the city. He felt our scenes resonated with authenticity and brought back memories of his own unique experience there.

We'd later meet at the Atlanta Bread Company to discuss the screenplay in greater detail. When I arrived, it occurred to me that this was the first time I'd returned to the place since the night I'd gone over the outline with Altovise. None of the customers recognized her, so our visit went virtually unnoticed. The same wouldn't be true of this meeting. Geoffrey may have gained some weight and grayed a bit since his Cosby days, but he was still recognizable, and a few customers were staring at him. Geoffrey seemed totally oblivious to this, as he was, no doubt, accustomed to it.

"We're on a mission," I told him, just as I'd written in my letter. By now, I knew that our story was extraordinary and I wanted to explain what we hoped to accomplish. Although I'd started without a clear direction, by the time I finished the first draft, I noticed something amazing unfold. When I framed the plot, I'd established an almost supernatural aura, one in which miracles could happen. The message was subtle but unmistakable: God is love and with love, anything is possible, because love always prevails. When I looked closely, I realized that this message, like a gentle whisper in the wind, echoed throughout our entire story. Here was a musical which was based on a miracle, and the story's creation actually represented one. The scenes came together so perfectly that they seemed predestined to evolve in just that manner.

During our conversation, Geoffrey mentioned that he'd once met Altovise, but it was only briefly, when she and her manager were in The Tuscany's parking lot. Tony had introduced himself, and then introduced Geoffrey to Altovise.

"He gave me his card," Geoffrey recalled.

I'm sure he did, I thought, but decided not to talk about Tony. Instead, we spoke about young people and the importance of making education a top priority. We wanted to create materials that sparked their curiosity and made learning a fun and rewarding adventure. There were too many destructive images permeating from the entertainment industry and too few messages that were inspiring and uplifting. I stressed how crucial it was for us to make a difference and to continue to promote positive role models, much like Bill Cosby had.

Geoffrey really admired Cosby, and as he spoke of the actor, I could see the pride he felt in having worked with him. He not only had a great respect for Cosby, but also for Sammy Davis Jr. Geoffrey mentioned that, when he was growing up, Sammy's autobiography was required reading in his school, and it made a powerful impression on him.

Bill Cosby had made a strong impression on me. I respected, not only the high standards and quality he'd brought to his artistry, but his commitment to promote higher education. For a while, I'd thought that Cosby might even be a potential partner. Why wouldn't he want to collaborate? Especially, since so many kids were in dire need of inspiration. The idea grabbed me so forcefully that I couldn't help but ask Altovise, "Don't you know him? Don't you think he'd..."

Before I could finish, however, her face turned sour, and she immediately shook her head.

"No," she said, her voice beginning to crack. "After Sammy died and I needed help, a friend asked Bill if he could give me some assistance, but he never did."

I wanted to say something, but couldn't find the right words. Altovise said that Bill had been close friends with Sammy, but that they'd never even spoken since then.

"He never helped me," she murmured in an unforgiving tone. "Not for all these years."

I nodded silently and added Bill Cosby to the list of subjects to avoid.

Altovise grew quiet as she thought back on those memories. I wanted to change the topic and lighten up the mood, but words still failed me, so I drove in silence.

I still admired the special quality of *The Cosby Show.* It was one of the country's most successful programs, and it brought many viewers their first glimpse of the lifestyles of professional African Americans. The producers assembled an incredible crew and the chemistry between the actors was magical. In my mind, it represented a hallmark in entertainment and a benchmark by which to gage my own work.

Without a doubt, I knew that Altovise and I had a remarkable story, so I wanted nothing less than the best for our project. We needed a talented cast that offered the same wholesomeness found in *The Cosby Show.* True, it wasn't my job to recruit or select the talent, but many films were packaged and financed because of the actors already signed onto the project.

That day, I tossed around these ideas, thinking of how great Geoffrey would be in the role of Calvin Langston, the amiable father in our story. In fact, during the last few weeks, I'd actually had him in mind as I fine-tuned the character.

Geoffrey was anxious to talk about Oaxaca. He explained that when he was young he'd actually moved there for a while with his mother and two brothers.

"Wow! That's incredible!" I replied, because I'd once entertained thoughts of living there, myself, but I rarely met anyone else who'd been there.

Geoffrey was just as amazed to learn of my experiences in Oaxaca.

"You're a lot like my mother," he laughed. "I really think you two should meet."

He added that she now lived in Connecticut, but I failed to mention that I was from the same state.

There were other interesting parallels which he brought to my attention. For instance, I'd described how our main characters played their guitars at the Zocolo. As it turned out, Geoffrey had played his own guitar at the very same square.

"It is a strange coincidence," I agreed.

What was really uncanny, were the events that had taken place during the past few weeks. I'd revised the plot to include a special journal kept by Nathan Langston, the brainy, adolescent we'd created. The entire story of the Langston's adventure is recorded in Nathan's writings. Geoffrey was taken aback by this twist, because when he was about the same age, he'd kept a journal of his own experiences in Oaxaca.

"Wow!" I said. "That's wild!"

"Would you believe it?" asked Geoffrey, "I packed the journal away about a week ago and I just shipped it to L.A." He was moving back to the West Coast to resume a full-time acting career.

"That's incredible," I said, stunned.

Geoffrey remarked that the strange coincidences gave him goose bumps.

"Me too," I replied.

In fact, there were so many that it was almost eerie. Nonetheless, I was thrilled by Geoffrey's interest in our project.

"I'm officially onboard," he said, then modestly implied that it wouldn't make or break a deal.

"That's great!" I responded, because as far as I was concerned, we wouldn't make a deal without him.

Geoffrey's wife, Josette, and their young son arrived around this time, and after we were introduced, she decided to order some lunch. Since we'd discussed nearly everything, I gave Geoffrey the latest version of our screenplay and told him I'd talk with him later.

I drove home feeling thrilled, like it was time to celebrate. Now, we'd received reviews from two outstanding professionals: a television writer who also produced hit shows, and an actor who'd performed in one of the country's top TV programs. They both felt we had a great story. So why had I been so worried? We had a winner.

Geoffrey was "officially onboard" and wanted to play the role of Calvin. I couldn't have asked for better news, especially since he and his family were moving back to L.A. If everything went well and we got a studio behind the project, he'd be readily available for the auditions. Only one word could describe the timing – "Perfecto!"

# 12

## AN UNHEALTHY SEASON

*May 2005*
*Sarasota, Florida*

When Altovise said she'd be back in a few weeks, Tracey never appeared to doubt this. Perhaps, it was because she had no other close friends in Florida and didn't take seriously the possibility of them parting. Of course, their living arrangement was less than ideal, but where else would she go, especially in her condition? Now, Tracey's most consuming thoughts were of her rapidly declining health and her desperate need for food and money. As she grew paler with each day, she gave little thought to what was happening in L.A.

About a month earlier, Tracey had experienced so much pain that Altovise had called a cab to rush them to the hospital. They'd spent the evening in the emergency room at Lakewood Ranch Medical Center, and Tracey said she was surprised by how attentive Altovise was.

Lisa was initially vague when asked about what ailed Altovise's roommate. At first she said, "abdominal pain," and then "women's problems" – that old fashioned catch phrase – and finally, she revealed that Tracey needed to have a hysterectomy. The problem was, she had no health insurance to cover it. What's more, she was in such bad shape there was no way she could earn much money.

When I stepped into Tracey's bedroom, I'd always pause. She was a chain smoker, and I couldn't imagine how she managed to breathe, for a thick cloud of smoke always engulfed the room. Frankly, I'd also smoked from time to time, but never in such close and stifling quarters. Tracey must have caught a glimpse of my pained expression, because she began to blow thick smoke rings up into the air.

"How can you breathe in here?" I asked, as I entered the dark room.

She mumbled some reply, but I didn't really hear her.

By this time, Tracey was bleeding profusely each day, which seemed to me like someone hemorrhaging. She spent most of her time in bed and was rarely seen outdoors.

When I did see her, she was always very pale. There was only one day that I recall that she got dressed and went out with us. It wasn't a fun outing, but a necessity.

Tracey's doctor recommended surgery in mid-June. In the meantime, Tracey had to apply for Medicaid and complete the process required to determine her eligibility. Since she lived with Altovise, but received no pay, she needed Altovise to confirm her status.

I drove the two women to a Child and Family service center near downtown Sarasota. There, they filled out the first forms. Tracey told me that once she was deemed eligible for food stamps, she'd have to sign the last documents. This paperwork was done at Sarasota Memorial Hospital, where I took them later that day. After she'd completed all the forms, we had lunch in a small café in the hospital. Tracey looked relieved. Now, all she had to do was prepare for surgery.

When Altovise left for the West Coast, I braced myself for a period of uncertainty. With her absence, I experienced an unexpected void in my life. There were fewer trips to the stores, banks, and libraries, and my life seemed strangely quiet. Still, I had to think positively about the advantages of Altovise working from L.A. She did have numerous contacts there, and I expected her to immediately jump in and start promoting our story. As a matter of fact, the more I thought of it, the more thrilled I was about our future. Exciting opportunities were just around the corner.

I'd been working around the clock and was a little frazzled, so it seemed like the ideal time to take a break. After all, the hardest part of the work was over, with only minor revisions to do on the script. Still, I was determined to help out in any way possible. Having contacted Michael, I thought I'd made substantial inroads to Disney, and his enthusiasm convinced me that our screenplay was perfect for their company.

Tracey may have missed the clues, but I was fairly prepared, in case several weeks passed and Altovise hadn't returned. Tracey may have actually ignored the warning signs. But, then again, even Altovise thought she'd be back. Instead, Barrett moved her into his small Reseda townhome, making space for her to sleep in his son's bedroom. I'd later wonder how such an awkward arrangement evolved. Were the contract talks delayed as one week slipped into another? I wondered how Altovise managed to handle all this. She hadn't said anything about where she'd stay. I just assumed that she'd visit a friend, or rent a room. I did recall one conversation, though, in which she mentioned a special occurrence that would take place.

May 16th was the anniversary of Sammy's death. Altovise said that, on this day, she and other family members always got together to remember him at his gravesite. Since this was an annual tradition, I knew she didn't intend to miss it.

"You know," she remarked, "Sammy wanted to live long enough to see our twentieth anniversary. And he made it, and then died a few days later."

I expected to be in frequent contact with Altovise, but back then she had no cell phone and it was hard to communicate. I assumed that she had visited Sammy's gravesite, and hoped that all had gone fairly smoothly. We wouldn't learn until later, when our certificates were mailed, that it was on May 16th that *A Detour to Mexico* was officially registered with the U.S. Copyright Office.

When I finally spoke with Altovise, it was not without a great effort. On my first attempt to call, I reached Indira, Barrett LaRoda's wife. After getting their number from Tracey, I knew to expect a cool reception. Indira sounded very cautious, and even after she got my name, hesitated to let me speak with Altovise. Each time I called, the woman said she was sleeping. I left messages, but was never sure if Altovise received them. More days passed, and since she hadn't phoned back, I became worried.

I called Michael Carrington and advised him that Altovise was in Los Angeles. I also briefed him on my concerns about her managers. If he was going to pick her up, he had to be prepared for a delicate situation. Altovise's managers weren't involved in, or even aware, of our project, but since Altovise was living at Barrett's home without transportation, she was pretty much dependent on him. That meant, there could be no discussions about the screenplay until they were safely away from his house. Michael was sensitive to the circumstances and assured me that he'd be discreet.

I also mentioned that Altovise wanted to write her memoir, but needed to accomplish a real triumph in her life. Michael thought that her autobiography would be compelling and certainly worth pursuing. He was anxious to meet Altovise and said he'd await her call.

I answered the phone one day and heard Altovise's voice.

"Alto! I've been trying to reach you!" I said, relieved.

I could hear the excitement in Altovoise's voice as she updated me on the progress of the contract talks. When she asked about what was happening on my end, I could tell from her tone that she was braced for a possible letdown. Our conversation revealed an issue that was more severe than I'd realized. Altovise was terribly insecure. She may have hoped for the best, but she didn't actually expect it. Her personal experiences had taught her more about fear and failure than about hope and perseverance. While she idolized her husband, and the value of his work and legacy, she was much less confident in the value of her own, and this was alluded to in the words that followed.

Altovise was ecstatic when she learned of Michael and Geoffrey's positive response.

"You're kidding!" she said, in disbelief. "They really liked it?"

"Of course," I replied, taken aback by her response. "We've got a winner!"

I told her that Michael looked forward to having dinner with her.

"Really?" she asked, as thrilled by the opportunity to meet him as he was to meet her. She took his phone number, and I told her to let me know how everything went.

Altovise called me right after her meeting with Michael, and I heard a level of exuberance in her voice I'd never heard before. She told me how charming he was, and how delightful to talk with. She was thrilled by how well the evening had gone. During dinner, they'd talked at length about our story and Michael had been very encouraging about the prospects for our screenplay. He'd also shared with her some helpful advice.

"He thinks we might consider using a biracial family," she said. "Maybe the mother could be Spanish or something."

"That's a thought," I replied.

Michael also explained the advantages of using an agent. Handing her his own agent's card, he encouraged her to give him a call.

"We really do need representation," stressed Altovise. I agreed, and said, "Well, why don't you give him a call?"

There was a pause.

"I'll give you the number," she replied, preferring that I contact him.

"Okay," I said, as I grabbed my phone book. I quickly entered Art Rutter's number and closed the book. Before hanging up, I said, "Guess what, Alto."

"What?" she asked.

"We're gonna' have a real Hollywood agent!"

We both laughed.

There was someone else whom Michael knew who could help us. Like Geoffrey, the popular actress, Raven Symone, had been a regular on *The Cosby Show,* only she was very young at the time. Since then, she'd always starred in high quality, kid-friendly projects, and her wholesome image had remained intact, which seemed like a rarity in Hollywood.

While writing, I used various techniques to help create the personalities of my characters and I initially clipped pictures of models from magazines to help me envision their features. However, I also had specific entertainers, like Geoffrey, who came to mind. Admittedly, when I began to envision Kimberly Langston, the teenage star of our story, Raven Symone seemed perfect for the role. This was only natural, since there were few black teen idols, especially actresses who could sing. The more that I thought of her, the more ideal she seemed for the part.

What's more, God had seemingly blessed me with a contact like Michael, who worked so closely with Raven, that it seemed almost too good to be true. It was great to have big dreams, but one also had to also be practical. I wasn't a magician. I couldn't pull another actress out of my hat, or another contact like Michael. I lived hundreds of miles from California, and being a true neophyte in the industry, I had to work with what I had. As they said, "Beggars couldn't be choosy."

Unfortunately, none of this mattered too much to Altovise, especially after I'd turned on the T.V. and she'd watched an episode of *That's So Raven.* Instead of being excited about an amazing opportunity, she saw only an actress who wasn't thin, and she was unimpressed. Not only did she feel that Raven was too heavy, but too mature looking to portray Kimberly. We'd created a cute, seventeen-year-old character, and Altovise couldn't see how this would work.

I understood where she was coming from and I was equally concerned about Raven's changed appearance. However, I subscribed to, yet, another adage: "Where there's a will, there's a way." The covers of the hottest magazines always touted the latest crash diets of the stars. So, what actress wouldn't trim down for a part in a movie?

Still, I decided to leave the issue alone for a while. Altovise was my partner and I had to respect her wishes.

Looking back, when it came to our screenplay, I was very much like a protective parent. I wanted only the best for it. The work had been grueling, exhausting, but it was necessary in order to lay the groundwork for a successful film. I wanted to offer the same wholesome virtues found in *The Cosby Show*. Now, here were two former *Cosby* stars that could bring that same quality to our project. Name recognition was important, as it helped provide a dynamic package to present to producers.

While, I didn't know everything about the film industry, especially on the investment side, I understood that we'd created a musical and it had to be relevant to be marketable. It had to have the right chemistry. That meant, great music and lively characters. An enormous amount of time was spent on the research, alone, to ensure that the scenes conveyed a feeling of authenticity. I wanted our audience to feel like they, too, were traveling through Mexico. It was challenging, but I prayed that I'd create the type of dialogue that resonated with truth and an overall message that was entertaining, educational, and inspirational. All the relentless writing, and rewriting, was worth it, because we had a special story.

# 13

## HOME ALONE

*Mid-June 2005*
*Sarasota, Florida*

**B**ack at Medici Court, there was nothing short of chaos. Lisa now called more frequently, as did Tracey, who needed more feminine pads, food, cigarettes, and money. Lisa and I would make periodic trips there, usually to drop off food. Sometimes Tracey would come out to the car, unfettered about being seen in pajamas. I remember making a delivery from Taco Bell and thinking that she didn't have much longer to wait for her surgery.

Tracey thanked me for the meal and the small change I'd given her.

"Hang in there," I said.

I also began to hear more frequently from Altovise, who now carried Indira's old cell phone. I noticed a drastic difference in her tone, the first of many occasions when her speech would be slurred. Altovise often sounded disoriented, and when Tracey's name came up, she'd go into a tirade about how her roommate hadn't helped out and how she was a free-loader. Altovise's mind was poisoned with anger and alcohol. She was irrational, and terribly unhappy. There was no point in asking how the contract talks were going, or anything else. She was not in the mood to discuss them.

Even when Altovise was sober, something was very wrong. It was uncomfortable for her, living in Barrett's home, but she didn't have the means, or wherewithal, to leave. So, she shared the cramped quarters with her manager, his wife, and their two young children. Although Altovise spoke fondly of the kids and managed to endure the lack of privacy, a few years later, she would admit that it felt like being "imprisoned."

Uncomfortable as she was, it was nothing compared to the horrible predicament of her roommate. Tracey's surgery was scheduled for June 17th, at Lakewood Ranch Medical Center. It was finally getting closer to that date. Bleeding profusely, she was in miserable shape. Not only was she flat on her back, but now, without Altovise's assistance, virtually, flat broke. I learned from Lisa that Tracey desperately needed money, and considerably more cash than the few bills we'd dropped off. They were behind in their rent.

When I spoke with Lisa, I finally asked, "Well, who's responsible for paying it?"

She hesitated, unsure, herself, of exactly how it was handled. We gave Tracey what we could, but it definitely wasn't enough.

I'd planned to visit Tracey following her surgery, but about twenty-four hours prior to her admission to the hospital, she was forced to vacate their apartment. They were officially evicted.

Lisa rushed to their place to get Tracey, and as many of her belongings as they could gather. Then, she and her husband, Marc, hastily cleared some space for their new houseguest. Meanwhile, Tony wasted no time in clearing out the rest of the apartment, stashing Altovise's things in his garage, and then, in a rented storage room.

During the following hours, Tracey agonized over her situation and tried to weigh her options. She and her parents were not on speaking terms, and her eighteen-year-old-daughter lived in another state. She had no close friends or relatives in Florida, and the reality began to slowly sink in; she was facing major surgery, alone.

As the time passed, the options narrowed. Tracey had to finally make a decision. Lisa and Marc offered her a place to stay, but in the end, she decided to cancel the surgery. She didn't want to impose any further. Instead, she began to make plans to travel to Oklahoma, or Chicago, where she had friends.

I felt very hurt for Tracey, especially after all the preparations she'd made. I wondered about the safety of even traveling in her condition. Years later, I'd also wonder why I never attempted to pray with her or, at least, talk about things that really mattered. True, she always laughed at me and probably thought I was like *The Flying Nun,* or, in our case, *the driving nun.* Still, during those solitary hours, when she was virtually a captive audience, I could have shared something more about my faith.

Lisa and I were initially baffled by the episode, but eventually, we both arrived at the same conclusion: it all seemed a bit too orchestrated, like a spring cleaning project that was efficiently carried out. The timing was so synchronized and smooth that it gave me chills. Tracey was effectively removed from the picture.

The more I thought of this, the more depressing it all seemed. I had tried to call Altovise, and tell her what was happening, but it was difficult to reach her. Then, I remembered one of our last conversations. She'd phoned from the home of a woman whose name I could scarcely make out. Altovise was disoriented and her voice was muffled. It was startling, because I'd never spoken with her when she was in such bad shape.

Altovise actually left the phone for a moment, and I heard her welcome someone into the room. Then, she returned to tell me she was going out with her stepson and his mother-in-law. Altovise gave me her friend's number, then she was gone.

In an effort to find Altovise, I called her friend. As the phone rang, I began to feel anxious. I didn't know if I'd been given the right number, or not, and I wasn't even sure of the woman's name.

I heard someone's voice as they answered the phone.

Stuttering a bit, I asked, "Are you Marilyn... or Mary Ann?"

Somewhat cautiously, the woman said, "Yes."

"Are you a friend of Altovise's?" I continued.

Again, she replied, "Yes."

I identified myself, and told the woman that I was trying to find her.

She advised me that Altovise's mother had died and she'd gone to New York for the service. The woman didn't know how long she'd be away, so, I thanked her, and after hanging up, I went directly to the store to buy a condolence card.

Altovise finally called, but again her speech was slurred. Her thoughts were erratic. At first, I had trouble understanding her, but when her words came together, the message was pointedly clear.

"Tracy owes me a lot of money…" she said, her voice rising sharply. ". . . for the rent."

I was stunned, for she sounded so unlike herself. What kind of state was she in?

"Alto…" I began, but it sounded like the phone went dead.

"Alto, are you there?"

I began to appreciate the seriousness of what I'd heard and witnessed. Had I written Altovise's story, this would have marked the end of the Sarasota chapters. These upsetting developments represented the last vestige of her aborted plans to rebuild her life in Florida. It was hard to believe, but within only a few months, the Bojangles Dance School and the plans to buy a new home were relegated to a part of her past. Likewise, her apartment at the Tuscany, and the troublesome roommate she'd left behind, would no longer have any relevance. With Mrs. Gore's death, there were no remaining reasons to start over in 'the sunshine state.' For all practical purposes, Sarasota was now history.

Altovise's life was certainly tumultuous, but I remained hopeful – even after this crisis – that she'd regain some degree of control over it. I found comfort in knowing that we were still moving forward with a meaningful project, and I assumed that the worst was behind us. After all, what else could go wrong?

# 14

## GO WEST YOUNG WOMAN

*August 2005*
*Indian Wells, California*

Initially, I'd made no formal plans to visit Indian Wells, California, but there I was, on a United Airlines flight to Los Angeles, with my daughter, Sandra, beside me. Altovise was indirectly responsible for the sudden invitation I'd received from Gloria Searls, an old family friend. Gloria was a brilliant, lovely, and self-possessed woman whom I admired for her ability to get things done. She'd always had and pursued big dreams and actively inspired young people to do the same. When she heard that I was working on a writing project with Mrs. Davis, she insisted that I come and help her write her own story. I agreed, since I was heading to the West Coast later that month, to have a meeting with our agent.

During the 1970s, Gloria was widely known for her outstanding accomplishments in the field of education. She was the first black woman to open private schools in swanky areas such as Beverly Hills and Palm Springs, as well as several other locations. They were collectively known as The International Children's Schools, and they attracted distinguished figures such as casting director and producer, Reuben Cannon, and Bill Cosby, both of whom she said were on her board of directors, and had registered their children at one of her facilities.

Gloria and Bill had been close friends for many years, and she'd written some of the episodes of his *Fat Albert* series, years before. Playboy mogul, Hugh Hefner, hosted major fundraisers for her, and I'd later see numerous photos of her students posing beside Bill and Huge on the sprawling grounds of the Hefner estate.

Gloria was proud to advise me that supermodel, Tyra Banks, had attended her Pico and Thurman schools, and there were even a few well-known faces who'd once worked for her before their careers took off. She said, one such staffer was Denzel Washington. The star, Ben Vereen, had performed for one of her fundraisers, and I'd personally met Bill Cosby's brother, Bob, who was a teacher at her Pico location. If that wasn't impressive enough, Gloria would play an old videotape of a young correspondent named Oprah Winfrey, who, in a 1988 news feature, covered one of Gloria's schools.

I remembered my last visit with Gloria, back in the mid-1980's, when she was near the peak of her career. I'd recently married, and was considering moving to Los Angeles to take a position at one of her schools. Gloria's hectic lifestyle was mind-boggling. Obsessively driven, she was the quintessential workaholic. She barely took time to sleep at night and was always working on piles of documents strewn across her bed. This led to hair-raising moments when Gloria was driving, as she often fell asleep behind the wheel. I decided that guardian angels hovered over her, or that her Mercedes Benz was wired with an auto-pilot feature, because she always managed to maneuver around the curvy cliffs of Bel Air to get home.

Gloria's first husband, Captain Fred Hutchins, was one of the legendary pilots known as the Tuskegee Airman, the first African Americans to serve in the U.S. Army Air Corp. I imagined that Gloria and Fred were probably twin spirits, for, both, were trailblazers who'd explored new frontiers. While Fred's most significant battles were waged while flying over the European skies, Gloria had fought to overcome various barriers in the field of education.

Twenty years had passed since my last visit with Gloria, and during the long flight, I wondered if she'd changed much over the years.

I'd long been divorced and my priorities had dramatically changed. Instead of my former husband, I was now accompanied by my seven-year-old daughter.

I gazed out over the clouds, hoping to get some sleep. I hadn't been to bed the night before, but, I still couldn't rest. Several questions flooded my thoughts. How would I work with, both, Gloria and Altovise? How far was Indian Wells from L.A.? How would I juggle my responsibilities? Altovise and I were going to meet with our agent, Art Rutter. I wondered what it would be like to work with him.

When Gloria opened the door to greet us, I was taken aback by how much she'd aged. Her severely curved spine had diminished her tall, regal figure so much that it looked painful for her to stand straight. She wasn't dressed to receive company, but this didn't matter, since we were practically family. Still, I was shaken by her disoriented appearance. It's doubtful that she fully appreciated what any of us wore. Having had diabetes for many years, she was now considered legally blind, and could only see the outlines of our figures.

Sadly, as I looked at Gloria, I realized the past years hadn't been kind to her. I'd heard that things had taken a downturn and that she'd lost her schools, but I'd never expected anything like this. Her appearance and circumstances had changed so dramatically, that it felt like I was introducing Sandra to a stranger. Where was the woman I'd known?

The atmosphere was dismal, even for an adult, so I was amazed by how well Sandra adapted to Gloria's home. Despite the affluent area in which she lived, there was an overwhelming feeling of destitution and loneliness. It was obvious that she suffered frequent periods of confusion, and didn't see the spilled coffee on the floor, nor the wall which was damaged when she'd tried to cook.

As I walked through the kitchen, I wondered, what had happened to the vibrant woman I'd know, and what had become of her schools? I never knew all of the details, but apparently, Gloria made a couple of imprudent business deals, mortgaging her home and other properties. Whether, it was simply bad timing, flawed planning, or a combination of the two, this would prove to be disastrous. As Gloria watched her business begin to crumble, she tried to unload some of her holdings. I understood that she shifted ownership of one school to her son, but he'd ended up losing it.

Gloria said that Bob, Bill Cosby's brother, wanted to buy one of her other schools, but when he approached Bill for help in financing the deal, his brother declined. Gloria never got over this. She still bitterly complained about this decision. According to Gloria, Bill said that his brother needed to make it for himself, just as he had, and "not look to someone else for a handout."

"That man worked hard," said Gloria, angrily. "And nearly every day, after work, he'd lift up his hood, not knowing if his car was going to start!"

I was struck by how much Gloria and Altovise shared in common. They'd traveled in similar circles, and known some of the very same friends. They'd both even approached Bill Cosby for help during the most desperate points of their lives. The two women had known what it was like to have millions at their disposal, only to experience the devastating tailspins that sent them spiraling toward obscurity. Now, they'd both resurfaced to tell their stories, but like survivors of a downed aircraft, they were still dazed from the crash.

Like Altovise, Gloria always perked up whenever she was around children. After all, it was her love for them that led to her strides in education. When she was with Sandra, she became much more engaging and her thoughts were more lucid, especially when we went on various outings.

For a young girl, Sandra was extremely protective of Gloria, and it showed whenever we were shopping. I'd pull up to the front entrance of a store, and she'd jump out and extend her hand to help Gloria get out of the car. Then, she'd hold Gloria's purse and guide her into the store. Sandra seemed to bring out the best in her, especially as they chatted together.

"Now read the ingredients on this label," Gloria told Sandra, handing her a pint of yogurt.

Sandra would comply, carefully reading each ingredient.

"What's the sugar content?" asked the former educator. "And the fat?"

After Sandra had answered, Gloria would think for a moment.

"No, better put that back," she'd say, when a product was unacceptable. "Check for another one."

Late one night, Gloria wanted to talk with me about Sandra. "She's an extraordinary child," she informed me. "And I've seen many. You need to have her IQ tested."

I promised Gloria that, once we were settled, I'd definitely look into it.

Gloria often brooded as she walked through the house, remorseful over the episodes in her life when people had betrayed or stolen from her. I tried to steer her thoughts toward happier days, and the highlights of her career, but the dreadful memories always took center stage.

Gloria constantly complained about a man – she called him her driver – who was always stealing from her.

"Why don't you just get rid of him?" I asked.

"These things always happen," she replied. Theft was commonplace, said Gloria, especially amongst senior citizens in affluent communities. I found myself scratching my head, totally baffled. I couldn't understand why she'd put up with that. She could barely see, which made her more vulnerable.

I suddenly had memories of a similar problem that Altovise experienced around the time of Sammy's death, when their employees reportedly stole valuables from their home. Of course, there were also the more recent incidents that had taken place in Sarasota. It was all very confusing to me.

"You shouldn't be here alone," I said, knowing that she didn't agree. "You need to find someone, preferably a woman, whom you can trust to take care of you."

Gloria wasn't ready to hear that, or any other overtures about settling down. She still wanted to accomplish a number of dreams that she had – and she always dreamed big – only now, she needed someone else's arms, legs, eyes, and abilities, to fulfill them.

I tried to give Gloria some assistance, but I hadn't traveled across the country to seek financiers for land acquisitions, write contracts for properties, and complete the legal documents for a limited partnership. Once again, I was falling into the habit of chauffeuring, as Gloria needed rides to do her banking in the morning, then, shopping and bill paying in the afternoon. When we finally got home, I had to fix meals, open the mail, and search for documents buried under countless stacks of files. It was a catchall type of role which amounted to tackling almost everything that came to Gloria's mind. Too often, those thoughts revolved around legal matters, and it became increasingly evident that she also wanted me to help with a lawsuit in which she was entangled.

The dual responsibilities of keeping up with a sympathetic, but restless, seven-year-old, and the hourly requests of a demanding elderly woman were extremely taxing. Gloria's penchant for midnight projects had remained unchanged, and around this time, when I was too exhausted to even sit up, she'd insist that we work on her book.

Additionally, Gloria's air conditioning system was malfunctioning, and after nights of sweating in an overheated bedroom, then needing a fur coat to use a freezing bathroom, I caught a strange case of the flu. It seemed to grow worse by the hour.

One morning, I had to face the truth. I couldn't stay there any longer.

I finally told Gloria, "I can't run errands all day long, entertain a child, cook, and then work on your book throughout the night. I don't have that type of stamina."

I hated to disappoint Gloria, but the book project, itself, was problematic. I couldn't bring myself to write about all the disturbing things that she'd endured. It wasn't that I didn't believe her. On the contrary, I knew more than I cared to. She'd lost nearly everything that she'd devoted a lifetime to building, and a plethora of tragic memories had stolen the grandeur from all she'd accomplished. Now, bitterness replaced the brilliance in her eyes. So, she lived there, all alone, in her own private hell.

"You have to refocus," I told her, "So you can deliver a positive message." We couldn't write a chronology of her legal battles, past and present. Who wanted to hear of her grudge toward those who'd betrayed and stolen from her?

We had go back and concentrate on the significance of her life and the transforming role she'd played in the countless lives that she'd touched – those of her students. In the end, this was the only thing that mattered.

Gloria's perceptions, however, were clouded. She couldn't appreciate the fact that, just one changed life, alone, was more significant than a building. If just one young girl – like Tyra Banks – was inspired to feel that she could accomplish anything, how many other lives had Gloria touched? This was the essence of her life, the real heart of her story, not the wreckage of her empire. She'd made a tremendous impact on the world, and changed it for the better. She needed to know it was okay to rest. She'd already done enough.

As I drove toward the highway, I felt torn inside. I travelled to Indian Wells, hoping to celebrate the accomplishments of an amazing woman. When I left, about a week later, I departed with a deep sense of sorrow in learning how tragic and complex her life truly was. Perhaps, part of the sadness was in sensing that it was the last time I'd actually see Gloria. She died during the winter of 2008, in her hometown of Atlanta, Georgia.

# 15

## THE SUN OVER SANTA MONICA
## BOULEVARD

*Week of August 16, 2005*
*Beverly Hills, California*

As I drove along Route 10, pulling tissues and blowing my nose, I began to wonder if I had something more than just the flu. My chest was so congested that I could barely focus on the road. Before I knew it, I'd depleted two boxes of tissue and had to buy more. It was an ideal time to stop, though, since I needed to call Altovise and let her know that we were on our way.

We were scheduled to meet with Michael Carrington and Art Rutter the following morning at a restaurant in Beverly Hills. In the meantime, we'd check into a small inn located only a few blocks away. Altovise actually knew the owner, who said she'd give us a special discount on our rooms. This sounded great, because I was on a very limited budget.

I thought we'd spend the evening in the library preparing for the meeting. I knew Altovise was feeling anxious, especially about discussing the specific details of our story. She'd forgotten some of the characters. No problem, I thought. I'd just give her a short briefing to refresh her memory.

At that moment, I needed a little help, myself, at least, with the directions. I hadn't had time to fully map out my route. I knew how to get back to L.A., but I wasn't sure of how to get to Reseda. Altovise was still living there with Barrett, and I was going to pick her up from there.

"Alto, can you give me directions from Route 10?" I asked, since the map from the car rental company wasn't very helpful. Altovise told me which highways to use and the exit that I should look for.

"Okay, I'll see you soon," I told her, thinking we'd be there in another hour, or so.

About two hours later, I called Altovise again. I couldn't find the exit she'd recommended, so I'd turned off at another one. "Are you sure I'm going the right way?" I inquired.

"No," she said, in an odd voice. "You should be going the other way."

"Oh," I replied and turned the car around. It was time to find a gas station and get a larger map. I was tired of going in circles.

It was dark when I finally found Barrett's street. It was located in a densely developed neighborhood, not far from one of the main boulevards. Despite this, I had missed the connecting street and wasted more time, as I continued to circle the area. Eventually, with Altovise navigating over the phone, I reached the right block. I parked my car near the gated entrance to a townhouse community, and as Sandra and I walked toward the gate, I spotted Altovise walking on the other side of it. We greeted each other, and after giving Sandra a big hug, she led us into the house.

Although Barrett and his family were out of town, I felt a little nervous. I'd heard so much about him, I was even intimidated by his home. Once inside, however, I was surprised by its size. While it was an attractive unit, it didn't seem well suited to accommodate a long-term guest.

I looked around the small living room and glanced at the black leather furniture. Something in the corner caught my eye. It appeared to be a shrine of some sort, with a picture of a man – a religious leader – positioned in the middle.

Altovise noticed that I was staring at it, but made no attempt to explain. She simply mentioned that she thought Barrett's wife was from Sri Lanka.

"Oh, like my ex-husband," I said, then nodded.

"Would you like to see the rest of the house?" she asked, with a slight slur. "Sure," I replied, taking a moment to look at her. Despite our delayed arrival, Altovise was unprepared to leave. She hadn't even started packing, which she mentioned as we climbed the stairs.

We walked toward a bedroom on the right.

"Where do you sleep?" I asked. "Right here," she replied, as she opened the door. It was Barrett's son's room.

Altovise then showed us his daughter's room and the master suite.

When we returned to the first floor, I helped Altovise pack her bags. She was not moving very fast and seemed oblivious to the time. I decided it was futile to try to study the materials. She wasn't in the right condition to read and absorb anything. Besides, it was getting late, and we all needed to get some dinner and some rest. I also needed some medicine. I was sweating with a fever.

I was thankful that Sandra had only suffered from a mild cold, and it hadn't developed into anything like my flu, because by the following morning, I had no voice. How ironic, I thought. I'd had countless illnesses in my lifetime, but only one other occasion when I'd developed laryngitis. Now, as I prepared for one of the most important meetings of my life, I couldn't even speak.

"This can't be happening," I whispered.

Thankfully, Altovise was in good spirits that morning. Her room was adjacent to ours and she knocked on the door early, to make sure we were up. I nodded, and smiled at Altovise, thinking, ready or not, the ball's in your court.

As we strolled through the lobby of the Hotel del Flores, we were greeted by the owner, an older, attractive black woman whom I'd met the previous night. I hoped to have an opportunity to talk with her about her inn, but that would certainly have to wait. The old art deco theme intrigued me, and I wanted to know more about its history. Altovise said that she'd owned it a long time, and from time to time, she'd considered selling it. That would be a shame, I thought, because it had so much potential. Obviously, it had seen better days, and I guessed that its heyday must have been around the 1970s, but it still retained a certain degree of charm.

When we arrived at the meeting place, the three of us laughed. It was so close to the hotel that we could have walked there faster than it took to secure a parking space. The Farm, a trendy Beverly Hills restaurant, was only two blocks away. I'd later regret having moved my car from the safety of the garage, especially since it was already paid for.

Michael and Art arrived together, and their appearance would have summoned anyone's attention. Michael, who was somewhat studious-looking, was wearing a cap sporting his show's name, *That's So Raven.* Since that was Sandra's favorite program, she was instantly charmed when Michael handed her a poster of Raven Symone.

"Wow," I laughed, trying to get my voice back. "How did you know that's her favorite actress?"

Art was more discretely dressed, and yet, his hawkish features and prominent ears, drew attention to his shaven head.

Both men were very excited to meet Altovise, and we all settled around a table in the middle of the restaurant.

This was the first time that Michael had seen Sandra, and he said she reminded him of his own daughter. I had asked about her attending the meeting and he was adamant that she come along. He had a wonderful way of engaging Sandra, even without speaking directly to her.

On our table was a long paper tablecloth, and as we talked, Michael doodled on it with his pencil. Sandra giggled when she recognized the character he'd drawn. It was Bart from *The Simpsons.* I whispered to Sandra that Michael had once written for the show, and her smile grew still broader as she watched him.

My fever made me uncomfortable and I was perspiring, although the room wasn't warm. I tried, however, to communicate, and urged Altovise to jump in, and contribute to the conversation. However, it was Michael and Art who did most of the talking.

I tried to express how excited we were about our story, and they nodded and were very complimentary. Art, however, said that he wondered if it was too nicey-nice. He explained that America's youth were very sophisticated, and he wasn't sure if they had an appetite for musicals and if there was a real market for them.

Stunned, I was now speechless for another reason. I believed just the opposite about musicals. I thought they were popular again, especially with young people, and felt the current trends supported it. So, I was caught off guard. I wasn't exactly sure of what he meant.

Michael was much more encouraging, and began tossing around ideas about who might star in the film. Both men agreed that the performer, Bow Wow, would be perfect for a role. Altovise and I smiled, though we, both, were thinking, "Who?"

I mentioned that Geoffrey Owens loved our story, and wanted to be considered for the role of the father. Art immediately frowned, and cautioned me about trying to usurp the decision of a producer. He wasn't supportive of the idea of trying to force any actor on the project. A preference for an actor, he said, could stall the contract process. I continued to listen, silently.

Art mentioned a couple of prospects he'd like to approach, and asked us if we minded if they arranged for someone to "shepherd" the writing and production of the project. Once we understood what he meant, Altovise and I looked at each other, then nodded in agreement. Sure, we thought. We wanted the input of experts in the field, so we welcomed this type of involvement. I studied Michael's expressions to see if he agreed with this approach, but at the moment, he was hard a work. His pencil was constantly moving, and he continued sketching until he'd finished the last member of the Simpson family. Sandra was thrilled, because each character looked just as they always appeared. I was surprised. I didn't know he was also an artist.

To this day I can't say what the food tasted like, for I barely touched my breakfast. It all looked fabulous, but I was too nervous and distracted to eat. I used all of my energy, just trying to speak.

At the table, I'd handed Art the latest version of our screenplay. At that point, he requested four additional copies. I was somewhat surprised, because I imagined that he'd have a secretary, or assistant, who could make copies for him. But, I immediately agreed to deliver them later, and planned to go directly to a business store to make them.

Art said that he wanted to show our screenplay to The Jim Henson Company, the original creators of **Sesame Street** and **Elmo**. Although, in my opinion, our story was geared toward an older audience than theirs, I was agreeable to approaching them, as well.

While we were talking, a woman sitting nearby recognized Altovise and quickly rushed over to hug her. She was a tall, attractive blond and very friendly. Altovise introduced her to everyone, and afterward, told us that she was singer Kenny Rogers' former wife.

Michael and Art joked about how many people came to The Farm to sign T.V. and movie contracts, and speculated about the percentage of writers who actually clinched the deals. I smiled as they chuckled, wondering where we'd stand in those calculations.

Around this time, Michael pulled out a camera and started taking pictures of everyone. I wished that I'd done the same, but he'd later send me the copies. A few minutes later, I remembered to go back to the car, because I needed to add money to the meter. Just before I finished, I noticed a note tucked under my windshield wiper. Someone appeared to have written down a phone number. When I returned to the table, I didn't think much about it and joked about having a secret admirer. We chuckled, thinking that he must have been nervous, because he'd written too many digits.

When we walked out of the restaurant, I felt that good times were ahead of us, but that sense of well-being lasted for only five minutes. When we crossed North Beverly Drive, my mouth dropped open. Someone had hit our car, knocking the mirror off the driver's side; it was dangling in the air by a cord.

Weird as it looked, I had no choice but to stick my arm out the window and hold the mirror up as I drove. The sight was like a remake of *The Beverly Hillbillies,* but I didn't have time to head back to the car rental office, at least, not until I'd handled everything else we had to do.

We drove to Santa Monica Boulevard, where Altovise had another important meeting over lunch. Now, some would have been embarrassed to drive up to the famous Friars Club, holding up a mirror in this fashion, but I didn't care. I had a fever, laryngitis, and more work to complete, so I had no time to worry about appearances. Besides, Altovise was attending a gathering there, and she couldn't be late.

We strolled down the hallway of a nearly windowless building, in an atmosphere soaked with history. The place was as much a part of Hollywood culture as Grauman's Chinese Theatre, and the various photos hanging along the walls testified to this. I was taken back through time as memories of countless old movies came rushing back to meet me. I gazed at the photos of legendary entertainers whose membership in the club dated back through several eras. This was their haunt, their own exclusive watering hole, and it dated back to around 1947, when comedian, Milton Berle, started arranging various get-togethers with other stars like Jimmy Durante and Bing Crosby.

As we were led to our table, it occurred to me that, within this room, countless celebrities had often dined, people like Frank Sinatra, Jerry Lewis, the Marx Brothers and Sammy Davis, Jr. Now, here we were, visiting with Sammy's widow. There was only one glitch. Sandra and I weren't actually having lunch with her. Altovise was led to another table where a number of committee members were holding a meeting.

Although our table was not far from theirs, I heard very little of their discussion. Altovise later said that they were considering a banquet in Sammy's honor and she'd offered to provide the wine as part of their fund-raising activity. Altovise had embarked on a new wine label that featured Sammy's image, and the company was based in Louisiana. The only issue they couldn't resolve was how the funds would be dispersed. Altovise felt that she should be paid a certain fee for the wine and the committee hadn't agreed to it.

I'd later realize that we'd had an opportunity to visit a historic place before it closed. During that same year, a lawsuit was launched against the managing group by the original New York Friars' Club, over its name. Only a few years later, the group was forced to rename their organization, and the location became known as "Club 9900." With its new name, it remained open for only a few months. After many years of serving Hollywood's greatest stars, the club reportedly closed in 2008.

Our next stop was a Staples business store, where I made copies of our screenplay, and then to the Shapiro-Lichtman Talent Agency, where I delivered them. Art's office was located on Beverly Boulevard, and I actually remembered more about the street than his agency. After I parked, I left Altovise and Sandra outside to browse around the shops. Once the copies were delivered, I went outside to join them.

I wanted to get the car back to the rental agency, but Altovise convinced me that we had a little time to window shop. Admittedly, I enjoyed this, until we were lured inside by the views of one store, in particular. I knew this was no ordinary boutique, and the name was familiar for some reason, but I couldn't remember why.

Within only moments, Altovise was admiring a stunning red dress she'd pulled from a rack.

"You know, this is Stella McCartney's shop," she said, dispelling the mystery. "You know, Paul McCartney's daughter."

"Oooooh," I murmured, stepping away from the racks. I knew my limits. I couldn't afford to get attached to anything in there.

"We'd better go," I said. "We can come back *after* we sell our screenplay!"

The next day, when we left the inn, we visited a nearby library to do some research. Altovise introduced us to her stepson, Jeff, who was employed there. He was very warm and cordial, and we all enjoyed talking with him.

I was planning to move to another inn, but Altovise invited us to visit with her for a few days. I'd never met Barrett, and felt awkward about staying in his home, but Altovise said it would be fine. Their family would be away for another week. So, rather than spend the money elsewhere, I agreed to pay Altovise, because I knew that she really needed it.

Sandra and I slept on the leather couches in the living room, but I decided against cooking in their home. Instead, we all went out for meals, and often used the time to go sightseeing. No matter where I went, however, I couldn't run away from the flu.

Altovise had just purchased a modest economy car, and would later buy a convertible Corvette. The cars were adequate, but a great step down from her Rolls Royce, which she said she'd sold "for nothing," and the Bentley she would have preferred. Still, it was a relief to finally have transportation. Despite the added notch of freedom, I noticed a certain degree of edginess in Altovise. In fact, I'd never seen her so moody. She was much less engaging with Sandra and sometimes even impatient. Although she showed us around the town and was anxious for us to see her old home, it never seemed to be the right time.

One afternoon, Altovise asked if she could take Sandra to a unit located across from us. She wanted to introduce her to a little girl named Troi. The two girls hit it off – although Sandra was a few years younger – and they spent the evening watching movies and playing video games. After we left, the girls would actually stay in touch with each other through letters, at least, for a couple of years.

Our last hours in California were extremely hectic, as I needed to repack our bags and ship boxes to Hawaii, where we were visiting friends that season. I thought there was ample time to return the rental car and relax at the airport, but I learned a terrible lesson about Los Angeles highways. While en route to the airport, I hit a major traffic jam and was forced to exit long before I reached it. Suddenly, I was maneuvering down a back street, unsure of where I was heading. I ended up calling one of the airlines to get new directions.

Sandra and I were, literally, huffing and puffing as we raced to catch our flight. In fact, I had to send Sandra, running ahead of me, just to urge them to hold the plane.

Soaked from sweating, and heavily congested with a nasal infection, I eased down into my seat. I knew I was tempting fate; the air conditioning was blowing down on me at full capacity. By the time we reached Hawaii, I was so ill that I had to go straight to bed, where I stayed for a couple of days. A few weeks later, after many cups of ginger tea, two visits to the doctor, and two different prescriptions of antibiotics, I finally began to recover.

# 16

## MINISTRY OF MIRACLES

*Late August 2005*
*Waimanalo, Hawaii*

In Hawaii, I felt reconnected to a life that I'd long missed. I'd lived in Oahu during the mid-1990's, and had always planned to return and resettle there. The natural beauty of the island's windward side distinguished it from any place I'd ever seen, and it was often depicted in lovely paintings and postcards. Nestled between the magnificent Ko'olau Mountain Range and the azure wisps of the ocean's waves, you could literally hear the winds whispering to you.

Once a fishing village, Waimanalo had retained the old rural charm of an unchanged outpost, and since many native Hawaiians still lived here, it offered a great deal of local flavor. While I always loved to explore the area, I never relished the idea of driving home after dark. To reach it, you had to navigate through, either, a steep mountain pass, or along a scenic, but curvy, cliff. There were only a few rustic-looking stores in which to shop for groceries, but that was okay with me. I liked the remoteness of a place that seemed hidden from the rest of the world.

At my friend, Sandy's home, I rented a small unit that her family had built, which was right off the kitchen. The guest room consisted of two twin beds, a desk, a T.V., and a door to the lanai. I thought of Sandy's home as a family compound, because the property also consisted of another dwelling, where her daughter lived with her husband and two sons. The place was located on a short street that led straight to the beach, in a neighborhood that ranged from old, wind-blown bungalows to million dollar estates.

Late at night, I listened as the winds thundered through the rafters and the waves crashed upon the shore, and took comfort in being close enough to the ocean to fall asleep listening to nature's unique lullaby. What a blessing, I thought, to live only a block from the sea. It was here, many years before, where I'd searched for real meaning in my life. I'd always loved Waimanalo Beach. It was here, while praying one day, that I'd accepted the fact that my life wouldn't be normal. While walking along the sand, I literally began my walk with God. Bumpy and twisted as the journey had been, the spiritual part had begun right here.

I was unsure of how long we'd stay in Hawaii, but I wanted my daughter to get to know Sandy – one of my closest friends – and her family. If all worked out, we'd be based here, and I'd continue working on my projects. In the meantime, there was something else I needed to do. I wanted to find a church and have Sandra baptized.

On August 29, Hurricane Katrina slammed into the Gulf of Mexico, hitting southeast Louisiana, and ushering in one of the country's worst natural disasters. I watched the news in horror, trying to believe the unbelievable, as the scenes of massive destruction and staggering death tolls unfolded. Each report grew more ghastly, as did the misery of thousands of homeless victims.

Perhaps, I watched too long, because the visions of the storm surge and its devastation began to unnerve me. I started having nightmares. My mind took me to places where I never wanted to go, and it camped out in the domain of all the "What if..." questions. "What if it happened here, too?" "What if we had a tsunami?" "What if the waves overtook us?"

I knew the Bible said that we should have no fears, but admittedly, I was worried. From that day on, I regarded the waves that I heard each night as threatening reminders of unfathomable suffering.

During the following days, I felt somewhat lost and unsettled, so I believed it was another stroke of providence when I found the Door of Faith Church. While riding on a public bus, I met a driver who shared the story of its founder, Mildred Brostek, and I was intrigued by the nature of her life. She was a Pentecostal evangelist who, in 1936, traveled from Florida to Hawaii to do missionary work. She'd recently died, but I was still anxious to attend her church, because Pastor Brostek was widely known throughout the islands, as well as Asia, for her amazing miracles. I'd seen miracles, myself, and felt a special calling to write about them, so I was thrilled to have an opportunity to learn more about the subject. I decided that, on the following Sunday, Sandra and I would visit her church.

Sandra started attending a school in nearby Kailua, and joined a local girls' soccer team. One of Sandy's granddaughters was the team captain, but she was initially so unimpressed with Sandra's athletic skills that I feared it would ruin their friendship. As the weeks passed, however, I watched Sandra evolve from being the slowest runner on their team to being very competitive. During their last competition, when a storm blew in, she just kept running, undeterred by the rain. She helped her team score the winning point.

I called Altovise and asked if she'd heard any news from our agent, but she hadn't heard from him. I promised to keep working to find a home for our screenplay and wrote letters to Art Rutter and a few producers whom I thought might be interested. I also kept in touch with Geoffrey, who'd resettled in California with his family. Every week, I would hope to hear good news. In October, however, there was still nothing to report.

Altovise gave me a friend's number and asked me to contact her. If I remember correctly, her name was Sue Damien. When I first called, I reached a voicemail with a profane message, and thinking that I'd contacted the wrong place, I quickly hung up and redialed. Same voice, same message. This time, I left my name and number, and she called me back a few days later.

I met Sue only once, the day when we arranged to have lunch together. Her maid, after greeting me at the door, escorted me to the living room, where she offered me a drink. "No, thank you," I replied, mesmerized by the view behind her. The huge room was completely open to the sea, extending an exhilarating feeling of being outside while standing indoors. The waves crashed onto the shore, violently, but beautifully, offering one of the most picturesque scenes I'd ever witnessed. The house, with its dramatic double staircase, offered a two-story view that was so breathtaking that I just stood there, spellbound.

Moments later, Sue's husband appeared from upstairs. I'd learn that he owned a real estate company, but I couldn't imagine him listing any property that was more stunning than theirs. After a brief chat, I was left alone for a few minutes to enjoy the room.

I had lunch with Sue at the Outrigger Canoe Club in Diamond Head, where she was a member. As we circled a table where some of her friends were seated, she took a moment to introduce me.

"Do you remember my friend, Altovise?" she began. "Sammy Davis, Jr.'s wife."

Two women nodded and turned to inspect me.

"Well, this is her friend, Pam, who's visiting Hawaii," she continued, and with a hint of humor, added, "She's entering the ministry."

All three women laughed and the woman sitting closest to Sue quipped, "Well, you won't save anyone, here!"

At that, they all laughed louder.

I felt embarrassed and I recalled how Altovise once said that her friends wouldn't agree with my views. I realized I'd made a mistake, at least, in speaking about them openly in her car. While driving to the club, we'd had a long talk and Sue had gotten right to the point. She said that, over the years, various managers and financial advisers had taken advantage of Altovise, and she was concerned about her well-being. She felt that her friend attracted unsavory con men and was often misled by them. I mentioned similar worries, especially considering what had recently occurred.

Sue questioned me thoroughly about the nature of our relationship. I didn't feel defensive, because I understood her concerns. As Altovise's friend, she wanted to know who I was, and where I was coming from, so I confided in her about the project we'd started. I told her about Altovise's desire to write her memoirs, but that it seemed premature.

I'd been very candid, because I wanted her to understand the type of work we'd undertaken, and why. In less than ten minutes, though, it had become the hot topic of humorous banter.

I was considerably more guarded when we spoke during lunch. I decided to let Sue do most of the talking. She spoke at length about her friendship with Altovise and Sammy. She mentioned that the couple had often vacationed with her on their visits to Hawaii. She'd known Sammy for many years, dating back to when he was young and heading toward superstardom. She told me that her father was one of the owners of a Las Vegas resort where Sammy performed, but during the early days, he wasn't even allowed to stay there.

"He slept in a trailer in the back of the hotel," she said.

"What?" I asked, stunned. "You knew him back during those days?"

"Oh, yes," she replied.

Sue was a striking older woman, who appeared much younger than her age.

Remembering their experiences, she said, "He wasn't always very nice to Altovise."

I mentioned that Altovise wanted to reach out to kids and promote education, just as Sammy had requested. This would also humor their friend.

"He didn't even like his own kids," she muttered.

Paring down the conversation a bit, she made casual chitchat about having dated one of the Beach Boys. I had noticed several of her friends' pictures back at her house, and wondered which one he was. She'd also known Duke Kahanamoku, the famous Hawaiian surfer and Olympic gold medalist. I was extremely excited about this, as I'd just watched a movie based on his life and visited a Waikiki restaurant which was named after him. Sue, however, didn't have anything too complimentary to say about, either, Duke or Sammy.

I thought Sue was just being contrary. After all, she'd confided that she and her husband were having a disagreement over an inheritance issue with his children, so I decided that she was simply in a bad mood.

While driving back to Waimanalo, however, I was still puzzled over two things Sue brought up. She'd asked if I'd noticed anything peculiar about Altovise, like a strange problem with her memory. To be honest, I hadn't. Other than the times when she drank, Altovise always seemed fine.

Then, there were Sue's parting remarks. She'd given some thought to Altovise's desire to write her autobiography. Just as I was leaving and heading toward the car, she said, "It wouldn't be safe for Alto to write her book."

"What do you mean?" I asked, startled.

"It just wouldn't be safe for her," she replied.

I wrote the minister of the church I'd attended back in Sarasota, and sent him some of my writings. I wanted to keep in touch and hopefully get some direction. I was feeling confused about where I was heading. Was I neglecting the work that God wanted for me? Was I putting my own objectives ahead of the ministry? Was it meant for me to come back to Hawaii? Or was I simply moving in circles?

There was a new problem and I wasn't sure of how to handle it. I'd always admired Sandy; she was one of my closest friends. Half Hawaiian and half Irish, she was stalwart and practical, loving and generous. In the true nature of the early Hawaiians, she was the strong matriarchal force in her family. The problem was, Sandy and her husband, Chris, were very wary of the Door of Faith Church. They had their own views about the miracles attributed to Pastor Brostek. Chris may have accepted Sandy's ruling of their home, but he didn't think too favorably about a woman leading a church.

They told me that Pastor Brostek was known as the "Magic Woman," and from their expressions, they were skeptical about what she'd actually performed. I understood exactly how they felt. For much of my life, I'd also discarded miracle stories. To me, they were purely figments of one's imagination and were often based on mere coincidences. That is, until I witnessed events that I couldn't explain in natural terms. Since I was fairly sure that I wasn't crazy, or, at least, not entirely so, these manifestations had somehow occurred.

For me, the subject of miracles wasn't just a passing curiosity. When I read a biblical passage that said we should tell about God's miracles and wonders, I accepted it as part of my mission. Still, I didn't understand very much about them, so I looked forward to meeting others who'd had similar experiences. Maybe, I'd finally learn how they happened and what they meant. Then, I'd be able to write intelligently about the subject.

Sandy and Chris tried to discourage me from visiting the church, but my mind was made up. On the following Sunday, I got Sandra ready and we started off to the Door of Faith. Sandy was surprised that I was still planning to go, and looked very strange as we headed toward the door. I didn't want to hurt her feelings or minimize the value of the fellowship at her own church, but I desperately needed to find my own answers.

Sandra and I couldn't see the church as we walked down the street, but we certainly heard the music. As we neared the building, it grew louder, and as the church came into view, we saw four women standing outside beside two long tables. Sandra's eyes lighted up when she spotted the cookies and drinks, and two women wearing long muumuus warmly greeted her.

"Good morning," said an older Chinese-Hawaiian woman, as she glanced at Sandra. "Would you like some cookies and juice?" The welcome was comforting to my daughter, because Sandra felt as nervous as I did. She'd had to adjust to several new experiences, and now, here was another.

I was surprised to find that the church was relatively small, but it was the building the congregation had occupied for many years. They were made up of believers of nearly every race and they all seemed to go out of their way to make us feel at home. From the moment that we walked in, people shared with us stories of how their lives had been redeemed, including a brother named Christian who'd defeated his addition to drugs.

It was an amazing gathering of people who, week after week, poured out their love for us and each other. Twice, we were given flowered leis to wear around our necks, and one of the grandmothers invited us on an outing with her grandchildren. When I asked about Pastor Brostek, one of the members lent me a book written about her life. I brought it home and immediately read it, and I was astounded by the miraculous nature of the Pastor's life. I found myself dreaming of producing a movie that was based on it.

I loved the church and was later pleased to have Sandra baptized there.

As the weeks passed, I began to feel restless with my life. I considered Pastor Brostek's accomplishments and wondered when I'd have my own. She's made a powerful impact, especially in the lives of young people, and converted many wayward youths into strong believers. I wondered when I'd move beyond my stalled efforts to do real ministry work? Was I even in the right place? I loved Hawaii, but something didn't feel right. I couldn't put my finger on it, but I felt like someone in limbo.

There was something else that weighed heavily on my heart. Years before, when I thought I was meant to build a church, I'd initiated steps to buy some of my grandfather's land in Alabama. When I heard that many of Hurricane Katrina's victims were left homeless, I felt depressed. I'd donated money, but I felt like I needed to do more. I'd learned that there were thousands of unused FEMA trailers in places like Selma, Alabama, and I thought of my family's undeveloped land in Coosa County, and considered the possibility of making it available to them. What if I stopped procrastinating and moved forward, clearing the land and letting them use it. The idea, at first, seemed rather remote, but if people came there, they might want to stay. And if they stayed, they might need a church, the edifice I'd once dreamed of building. After giving it more thought, I was sure that I'd gone crazy.

Still, I decided to contact FEMA, the government's Federal Emergency Management Agency. After numerous hours of reaching busy numbers, wrong numbers, and countless people who redirected me to countless others, I finally reached someone who, at last, took down my name and number. I couldn't imagine what it was like for actual hurricane victims who were desperate for help. It must have been, both, frustrating and frightening.

I'd decided that, if I finally contacted the right officials and they told me that they didn't need the land, I'd just chuck the idea. However, if FEMA thought the property was suitable, I'd keep working to make it happen. So, I kept calling. When I finally reached the right office, I was told that my idea had merit, and I was asked to provide them the details about the closest schools, utilities, and water. So, I began researching the area to determine the best ways to provide water, power, and other needed resources. I contacted the counties that had jurisdiction in the area to get estimates of the costs. Before long, I'd accumulated a large database of contacts and information. I learned so much about the area, that I was intrigued by the idea of living there.

Frankly, I'd never before liked the idea of going to Alabama, not even as girl, when we visited my grandparents. It was always too hot, and too "southern," and as my father said, I was "A real New England Yankee." I remembered, all too well, my parents' stories of lynchings and other graphic scenes of racial hatred in Alabama, so I always dreaded going there on summer breaks. Thirty years later, I was still wary of the state. In fact, when some of my relatives had raised objections to my buying the property, I figured it was a great excuse to back out of the deal. "Look, Father," I thought. "I tried to build your house, but they just wouldn't let me."

Nevertheless, I knew that, if it was meant for me to build some type of ministry there, I'd have to learn to adjust. After all, it wasn't like I was moving to Siberia or leading a missionary group through some war-torn country. It was just Alabama, and I could write my books and screenplays, even from there.

After praying about it for several days, I packed our bags and we headed back to Florida. As a co-purchaser with my mother and brother, I signed a contract – with owner financing – for approximately fifty-five acres in Coosa County, Alabama. When we closed on the deal in mid-November, I felt assured that, once our screenplay was sold, I'd be able to pay off the loan.

I contacted our agent, again, to see how things were going. There was no progress, so I considered the possibility of writing the book version of our story.

# 17

## HOLIDAY GREETINGS

*Christmas Day, 2005*
*Sarasota, Florida*

I called Altovise to wish her a Merry Christmas, and to talk about a serious concern I had. While doing research in a Borders Bookstore, I came across another biography about Sammy. Wondering if it was new, I picked it up and glanced through the pages. That's when something caught my eye. There was a reference made to his involvement with Satanism and I was immediately shaken. I quickly checked in another book and saw a similar note. I realized that this had been hinted to in other publications, but I'd overlooked it.

"No!" I whispered. "This can't be true!" I wasn't superstitious, but being a Christian, I was very worried. How had this affected Altovise? Were these stories true, or were they simply fabricated rumors that had lives of their own? I didn't know what to believe, but I had to address it right away.

I told Altovise that, if there was anything she'd been involved in that might have separated her from God's blessing, it was a good time to repent. I'd recently gone through a detoxification process that thoroughly cleansed the body and I compared it to this experience.

It was the holiday season, so I suggested: "Alto, let's start the New Year totally cleansed, free from anything that would block us from having a blessed and successful life."

It was a long distance conversation, so I could only gauge how Altovise felt from her voice. She agreed, however, and said it sounded like a good way to start the New Year.

I received a belated Christmas card from Michael. Enclosed were a few photos he'd taken of us during our meeting at The Farm. There was a great shot I'd taken of him with Art.

Oddly enough, Art was the only one I hadn't heard from, so I contacted him, again, to inquire about the status of our screenplay. Art said that he'd heard nothing back from any of the contacts he'd reached and that they hadn't returned any of the materials he'd sent them.

"That's really unprofessional," he said.

Art requested another copy of the screenplay, and just before hanging up, mentioned, again, his concerns about the marketability of a musical. After all, it wasn't like we'd written about the Jackson Five.

I felt confused and disappointed. While, it was true that musicals had suffered many years of decline, the tastes and trends had dramatically changed and there was something akin to a renaissance taking place. On this particular issue, Art's feelings were totally at odds with the messages I'd received from Michael, who'd stressed that the film industry was avidly looking for musicals, particularly the producers at Disney. Recording artists could be showcased in these films, intensifying the growing popularity of the genre. This was especially true after the overwhelming success of films like *High School Musical,* the coattails from which created a financial bonanza that included concert tours, music-related products and other merchandise.

In fact, Michael had stressed in a recent e-mailed message that it was an opportune time to pitch our story. He assured me that he was going to call Art and emphasize this point. I felt relieved, because I knew Michael was right.

# 18

## A TOUCH OF HUMOR

*April 2006*
*Sarasota, Florida*

I began to awaken at strange hours of the night. Another irresistible story idea kept nudging me for attention and I finally started to write it down. I'd thought of it many times, especially during that past year, and even discussed it with Dave Sullivan, an old friend who'd also toyed with the idea of writing screenplays. Around March, we got serious about creating the main character who, by then, we both knew.

Our basic story outline was formed by April, and it was so hilarious that I laughed uncontrollably each time I read it. The plot revolved around a hopeless gigolo who'd made a fortune out of swindling women. He could have been like millions of others, only his technique was extremely unique. I'd never written anything like this before, which is why I needed Dave's help in creating this adorable scoundrel.

It was true that Altovise and I brought Alex into being, but he was a much younger version of a Casanova- wannabe. This character was very different. He was a polished, professional con who was downright dangerous, when it came to matters of the heart.

I never thought that Dave resembled, or was sympathetic to such a character. However, he was brilliant in his ability to articulate, with authenticity, the character's motives, behavior, and expressions. He was frighteningly accurate in describing the character's personality traits, and he wasn't as timid as I was about using strong language. After all, this was an adult film, not one of my children's projects.

Dave's contributions were like the yeast in a loaf of bread. He offered much of his own personal insight into the inner workings of the predatory male, and it was always hilarious. Lastly, he also worked in the legal field, and the first scenes took place in a fictitious law school.

It was fun to finally work on a project together. We'd met many years before when we both were congressional interns in U.S. Senator Lowell Weicker's office. I have to admit, I was taken by his rakish charm and mischievous sense of humor. His handsome features and political interests reminded me of one of the Kennedys, at least, when they were young. In fact, I'd often joked about him eventually living in the White House. Over the years we'd remained good friends, and knowing my love for writing, he'd sometimes share his latest story ideas. It seemed inevitable that we'd eventually collaborate on a project.

I knew from the beginning, though, that I'd have to do the bulk of the writing. An Assistant U.S. Attorney in Connecticut, Dave had a very demanding position. He also had an active family life, so even when he wasn't tied up with work, he had considerable demands on his time.

Still, Dave managed to come up with some of the funniest dialogue we'd use, and the risqué twists he added made the material difficult to put away. He'd always make some witty, over-the-top remark, and I'd inevitably shriek, "Wait! Let me write that down!"

Before long, I decided to ask Michael to join us. We thought his input would be invaluable, as he'd had broad experience in writing comedy – from *The Simpsons* to *That's So Raven* – and had a wealth of insight to offer. The timing also seemed perfect for Michael since, during that winter, the production of *That's So Raven* had suddenly ended. In fact, the announcement of its last episode had seemed so abrupt that many were taken aback. Even, Michael, a writer and producer on the show, didn't have a clue that the program was going to shut down.

When he'd emailed me with the startling news, he mentioned that he was looking for another job. So, I thought this was a great opportunity for us to collaborate. Naturally, Dave and I were thrilled when Michael came on board. I looked forward to gaining valuable new skills and insight from both of my new partners.

I hadn't forgotten *A Detour to Mexico*. I'd just invested so much time and energy into it – as well as all my hopes – that I needed to recharge with something new and completely different. Although everything I created included a spiritual note, this one came with a zany edge to it. Even in the midst of adultery and debauchery, there was still room for miracles.

I knew I'd have to return to *A Detour to Mexico,* and finally complete the book version of the story, but in the meantime, I'd get this second project off the ground. Then I'd be in a better position to sell the first screenplay, and get the money needed for the land in Alabama.

That spring, Dave, Michael and I worked from our various outposts, emailing ideas back and forth between Florida, Connecticut, and California. It felt like we were partners in crime with a killer story that would knock everyone out.

# 19

## GUESS WHO'S COMING TO DINNER

*Early August, 2006*
*Sarasota, Florida*

Altovise came to stay with us for a few days, and I'd invited a couple of friends for a special dinner to celebrate her visit. In preparation, I tossed the fresh spinach and vegetables in a bowl, then crowned them with nuts for a vibrantly colored salad. A few minutes later, I removed a pan of shrimp and Spanish rice from the stove and pulled the flanks of steak rolled in seasonings from the oven. Since the bread was ready, I began to serve everyone's plate.

I forgot to make Altovise's serving smaller than the others, which I'd soon regret, for during dinner, she barely touched her shrimp and rice dish. My mother didn't fail to notice this and made a curt remark about Altovise's modest appetite. My parents, much like Depression-era pragmatists, believed that the adage, "waste not, want not," applied to everyone, no matter who they were.

As I cleared away the dishes, I listened to their conversation. It was a discussion led by Altovise, and it continued as I prepared the dessert.

"I once threw a kids' party for Sammy," she said, reminiscing about the occasion. "As a boy, he'd been a performer and hadn't gone to school," she reminded us. "And he missed having a real childhood with the normal birthday parties and everything. So, I planned a kids' party for him. All the guests were told to dress up like kids."

Although she'd mentioned the nature of Sammy's childhood before, it was the first time she'd spoken of this occasion. Her eyes were aglow and I was touched by the emotion in her voice. She must have tried to fill a vacuum that she sensed still remained in his life, something crucial that he'd been deprived of. Altovise laughed as she remembered the first guests to arrive.

"Most of them wanted to see who else was there before they'd wear their costumes," she said. "Sally Struthers was the first one to come fully dressed."

Altovise's description of her outfit sparked memories of my old Raggedy Ann doll. I'd seen the actress in various episodes of *All In The Family*, the phenomenally successful show in which Sammy appeared as a guest in 1972. In fact, the scene in which he kissed Archie Bunker, the infamous bigot portrayed by Carroll O'Connor, became one of the most historic television moments on record. Although Struthers portrayed a married woman in the sitcom, her character always came across as being more childlike than adult. So I smiled, thinking that it was probably easier for Struthers to jump into the mood than Altovise's other guests.

"Sammy was totally surprised when he got home," she said. "And at first, he didn't quite know what to do."

"What did he wear?" I asked.

"Well, obviously, he hadn't known," she replied. "He'd been at work. He just wore some jeans."

From her proud smile there was little doubt that her jamboree had been a success. Yet, within only moments, she seemed preoccupied by other thoughts. Perhaps, she was sifting through memories of similar gatherings. Whatever they were, she wasn't inclined to share them and I wasn't going to press her for details. We'd always operated this way, as though an unspoken agreement was established to leave certain things unspoken. By then, I knew some topics were just too sensitive to discuss.

When I gazed at Altovise, I still struggled to process what I'd learned. During her turbulent life she'd experienced such dramatic contrasts, they seemed incomprehensible. After spending time with her in Beverly Hills, I was much more familiar with the stark contrasts in her life, the two worlds in which she'd lived.

Under the safety of Sammy's wings, she'd soared to unparalleled heights, but after his death, plummeted to unspeakable depths. In Beverly Hills, the aura of wealth and glamour was so thick it was palpable. More than once, we'd driven unnervingly close to Rodeo Drive, the posh commercial strip where Altovise had often shopped. It was here that she'd casually spent mind-boggling sums of money.

After all, Sammy believed in having only the best. So, in the closets of their twenty-two room mansion were various mink and other fur coats, jewel-studded outfits, elegant gems, and luxuries too numerous to recount. As noted in Gary Fishgall's book, **Gonna Do Great Things,** their garage accommodated a his-and-her collection that included "A Mercedes, Rolls Royce, Jaguar, Ferrari, Dusenberg, DeLorean, a rare Cadillac station wagon, and a gold custom-made Stutz Bearcat."

They lived on top of the world, or, at least, the most glamorous part of it, and their dazzling lifestyle was anointed by royalty, dignitaries, and celebrities whom most people simply ogled at. The couple was infamous not only for hosting extravagant parties, but for rubbing shoulders – among other things – with some of the world's most influential figures.

To keep up this lifestyle, they incurred some heavy debts. Sammy, who'd established a long history of outspending his earnings, had always managed to catch up. There were often advances from night clubs, even loans from various mobsters and friends. Over the years, their financial problems had steadily mounted, as had the back taxes they owed to the Internal Revenue Service. This didn't appear to cramp their stride, though, and the rocking parties continued.

One gala, which the couple named their "Decade Party," was thrown shortly after comedienne Phyllis Diller joked about their financial problems on the air. The gathering was meant to dispel rumors that they'd squandered a fortune, and they initially planned to host only twenty-five couples.

Altovise, however, sent invitations to friends and acquaintances throughout the world – approximately four hundred people – thinking they probably wouldn't attend. That was a costly mistake. When a deluge of affirmative responses flooded in, she had no choice but to plan a larger party - a much grander, blowout party.

Instead of one catering company, they required a second, and rather than just one band, they hired two. No expense was spared, from the hors d'oeuvres and friendly valet parking to Altovise's silk dress and their exuberant floral arrangements.

Through the doors walked an array of famous guests that included Zsa Zsa Gabor, Muhammad Ali, O.J. Simpson, Rita Hayworth, Liza Minnelli and husband Jack Haley Jr., and countless others. When all the music and laughter was over, and the last guest had long gone, the final cost of the extravaganza would amount to approximately $75,000. It was one of Hollywood's most talked about parties, and the media's coverage of the event didn't escape the attention of the IRS.

Ironically, it was probably the Decade Party that inadvertently brought down the curtain at their home, closing a decade filled with extravagant galas and ushering in a period mired by financial and legal battles. It was a legacy that would haunt Sammy for the rest of his life, as the IRS would take aggressive actions against the entertainer and his business partner. When Sammy died, he owned the government over $5 million.

Although a considerable amount of the debt was resolved, Altovise told me that she still owed the IRS about $1.5 million. As I looked at her, I wondered how she'd handled the staggering figures, the pressures stemming from such massive debt.

With her perkiest voice, Altovise began to recount a funny scene she'd just recalled. "Sammy wanted me to be involved with the group," she said, describing the events at a fund-raiser sponsored by SHARE,

Inc. It was a non-profit group that raised money for developmentally disabled, abused, and neglected children.

"And each year I worked with them, and performed for the fund raisers. But, one year we decided to ask Richard Pryor to be our guest, just as long as he kept it clean. That was the deal. No dirty language."

Everyone leaned closer, as Altovise continued.

"Well, when he got up on the stage…" she continued, chuckling, "He immediately started cursing!"

She covered her eyes, much like she'd probably sheltered them that very day. Everyone burst into laughter, trying to imagine the audience's response. I recalled the riotous expressions of the late comedian and how outrageously funny he was.

Altovise seemed to be enjoying herself as she recalled numerous encounters with other celebrities. Charleston Heston, like many others, mused over the fact that she was so much younger than Sammy.

"They all called me 'the kid,'" Altovise remarked. It was obvious that she liked the nickname.

Altovise, who was then sixty-three, looked much younger than her age, and I couldn't blame her for relishing this. However, there were times when she'd startled me by suggesting that we were close in age. She was nearly seventeen years my senior, which was almost the same span of years the existed between she and Sammy. I simply remained quiet at those times.

The conversation shifted to Sammy's unique relationship with Elizabeth Taylor and Richard Burton. She told us of a secret affair that the famous couple began. I wasn't sure of which period she spoke of, since I knew very little about their on-again, off-again marriage. However, I assumed it was at the onset of their relationship, during, or immediately following the filming of the movie, *Cleopatra*. Before I could get some clarification, Altovise mentioned something that intrigued me.

"Sammy was the one who helped them get together," she said.

"What do you mean?" I asked, puzzled.

Sammy acted as a front man, she explained, something like a decoy of sorts.

"For a while, the studio didn't want Elizabeth to see Burton," she continued. "They weren't supposed to go out with each other."

Everyone seemed amazed that these legendary stars were forced to meet clandestinely. By now, however, I was beginning to understand how Hollywood worked. Years ago, it was common for powerful studio executives to impose strict moral standards on their actors, codes that they, themselves, didn't always uphold. Like brand names, they created strong images of various celebrities, and to ensure that they lived up to them, they monitored even the most intimate facets of their lives. The studios' policies reflected their primary concerns – their financial investments and profit margins. As for love, it was a sentimental thing, and best packaged for the silver screen, but not necessarily beyond it.

"Sammy would take Elizabeth out," said Altovise, "but it was just a cover, just a way to help them meet in secrecy. He'd pick her up in his car, and since no one thought anything of it, they weren't ever followed. But, then, he'd drive her straight to the place where she'd meet Richard."

"Wow," I said, imaging the adventures. "In some ways, it was probably very exciting."

What I didn't say, was that it was strikingly similar to Sammy's own ill-fated experience.

My thoughts reared back to the events in 1957, when Sammy got involved with the famous blond bombshell, Kim Novak. Different versions were written about how they actually met, as well as how they were forced to part, but the most dramatic episodes of the affair were documented with some consistency. By all accounts, it caused a huge scandal. During the 1950's, their interracial relationship was a major taboo, even for a black celebrity of Sammy's stature. In terms of Hollywood history, it served as a hallmark case. Never before had the studios confronted a sticky race and sex-related debacle, at least none that posed a crisis of such epic proportions.

Friends tried to warn Sammy of the dangers, because more was at stake than just his career. He'd wandered into forbidden territory. Unlike his relatively unknown white lovers, Kim Novak was Columbia Pictures' biggest star. Production chief, Harry Cohn, had virtually created her - the sultry image and all - and as Kim would later lament, he regarded her "as a piece of property." From the "property," the company had already earned approximately $10 million on their investment. Additionally, the actress was just completing Alfred Hitchcock's film, *Vertigo,* and with so much on the line, no one was about to free the golden bird from her cage.

Like most stars, Sammy and Kim were closely watched by the media. Just one day after meeting at a party, it was promptly announced in a gossip column. Despite the scrutiny, or perhaps because of it, they decided to meet the following night for dinner. Thus, began a secret love affair that was never quite a secret.

The couple did make gallant efforts to conceal their relationship, and Sammy enlisted the services of an old friend to help. Since Sammy couldn't be seen in public with the actress, it was often Arthur Silber, Jr. who'd drive Sammy's delivery and get-away-car. The strange ritual began that very first night, and would continue for quite some time. Sammy would crawl into the backseat, where he hid on the floor under a rug. When time to leave, at that synchronized hour, he'd dash out of Kim's home, throw himself into the awaiting car, and Arthur would speed off.

On some evenings, Kim would visit Sammy, wearing studio disguises such as gaudy wigs to mask her identity. Eventually, Sammy would rent a house in Malibu for their rendezvous, using another person to actually sign the lease.

Then, there was their last adventure, the one rumored to launch their impending engagement. It took place during the Christmas holidays, when they were visiting Kim's family in Illinois. By this point, Sammy was so stressed by the challenges in their relationship, that he'd become somewhat reckless. He succeeded, however, in arranging a leave from the Sands, the Las Vegas resort where he was booked, but only after pleading with Frank Sinatra, his close friend, who was also one of the owners.

Finally, Sammy and Kim managed to get together, but, in pulling off this holiday feat, they invariably attracted unwanted attention. They may have made a tactical error when they decided to buy train tickets back to the West Coast. On their return, the media hotly pursued the couple, and a dramatic search for them took place on their train.

Sammy executed a cleaver escape plan, exiting the train early and artfully dodging the paparazzi, but those suspenseful, Hitchcock-like scenes were just as intense as any cinematic footage that was shot.

The journalists weren't alone in flagging the couple's maneuvers. So had Harry Cohn, who vowed to put an end to the affair, and he reportedly called in the big guns to do it. In addition to enlisting Frank Sinatra to pull in the reins, he solicited help from a contact at the William Morris Talent Agency (which represented both artists). Like the Las Vegas resorts, many Hollywood studios were heavily financed and connected to the mob, and Cohn also supposedly contacted such heavyweights as the New York crime boss Frank Costello, and the racketeer Mickey Cohen, who was based on the West Coast.

The stories differ slightly, but a number of books concur that a frightening set of events unfolded. A very intimidating 'messenger' from one of these organizations visited Sammy, warning him that if he didn't stop seeing the actress, he'd have both of his legs broken, and lose his one remaining good eye. Sammy had lost his left eye during a car accident. There was also another demand: he was to marry a black woman right away.

Terrified for his life, Sammy quickly pulled out his black book and started riffling through the pages. He stopped only after he found the name and number he was searching for, that of a singer he'd once dated. Her name was Loray White.

Within hours, a very hasty business deal was formulated, and within a short time an agreement was reached. There's great uncertainty about the gift that Sammy gave Kim that Christmas, but less than three weeks later, Loray received from him a $3,000 Mink stole, an engagement ring smothered with diamonds, and a matching diamond and platinum wedding band.

On January 10, 1958, Loray White accepted the new life that Sammy offered her, this, despite the fact that he loved another woman, and that only hours after their wedding ceremony, he was so drunk and distraught that he attempted to strangle her. Sammy was so depressed that he showed signs of being suicidal. In spite of all this, and the New Year's unsettling kickoff, Loray assumed the role for which she was reportedly paid, and thus, became the first Mrs. Sammy Davis, Jr.

# 20

## COME OUT SWINGING

*Early August, 2006*
*Sarasota, Florida*

On Saturday, I drove Altovise to Publix grocery store to meet with Tony Francis. She told me they had some business to discuss, so I did some shopping while she waited for him outside. When I emerged, I spotted Altovise leaning over the passenger's window of a car parked in front of the store. She was talking with Tony, who was seated in the driver's seat, and they were having a heated argument.

I didn't want to embarrass Altovise, so I simply nodded as I passed, and took my groceries over to the car. I waited for a while, wondering how long they'd fight, and hoping the tension wouldn't escalate. After awhile I walked back to the store's entrance. I kept a respectful distance as their war waged on, but stayed close enough in case Altovise needed help. Admittedly, if the need arose, I wouldn't have had a clue of what to do. I just prayed that it wouldn't. The man glanced over in my direction a few times, but since it was a bad time for introductions, no one made any. When Tony finally left, Altovise and I walked back to my car.

Tony, she said, wanted her to pay him $2,500 before he'd give her the key to her storage room. Since she wanted her belongings, she'd finally paid him off.

"Well, at least I've got the key," she said, regaining some of her composure, and now we could get her things out of storage. I nodded, but the strange nature of their encounter had unnerved me.

On Sunday, I took Altovise to church, where I introduced her to the minister and several church members. Grover, a friend that I'd started dating, took us to lunch downtown, and while we were walking along Main Street, we ran into Robert DeWarren. He was then the director of the Sarasota Ballet, and he remembered my daughter, who'd been a student at the ballet school and had once performed with the company. I introduced DeWarren to Altovise.

"Do come to the ballet," he told her, and she happily agreed.

As we strolled along the shops, Altovise slowed down to occasionally glance inside. Then she noticed an attractive boutique where the door was left open and the sale sign looked inviting. "Let's go inside," she suggested, and we wandered in.

Altovise agreed with Grover that I desperately needed a fashion makeover. My long, full skirts made me look "like a square-dancer," he said. So, they picked out a rather snug-fitting, short skirt for me to try on, and within a few minutes, before I could protest, Altovise had purchased it. Thus, I'd begin to adopt a new approach to buying clothing, a change that pleased a number of friends who'd long dreamed of changing my "boring wardrobe."

While eating at Two Senoritas, Grover asked Altovise a pointed question: why didn't she manage her own finances? Stunned by the question, she stuttered as she raised a margarita to her lips and made an awkward attempt to explain. She needed someone to oversee the affairs of her estate, she said, especially the royalty payments that were coming in each month. Someone had to keep track of all the figures and the various details, and she wasn't quite ready to handle it all.

# 21

## PRAYERS AND ROUND TWO

*Early August 2006*
*Sarasota, Florida*

The following morning, I made a decision. Altovise needed more help than I could offer. Although I'd taken her to church, I felt compelled to provide her with more spiritual equipment, the source that I relied on for strength and direction. I brought her to a friend's home for an early prayer meeting. In this informal gathering, encircled in the intimacy of Janet and Jack Hoza's living room, a few women prayed over her until she eventually joined in. Before long, Altovise was "speaking in tongues" with the others. I wasn't sure if she understood what was happening or truly felt a stirring of the Spirit, but I believed that I'd done the right thing. I felt comforted in knowing that, afterward, she seemed to exude a deeper sense of peace.

Demons lifted or not, by late afternoon, Altovise's journey toward redemption would be vigorously tested. Within a few hours, we'd have another encounter that, like providence, seemed predestined to happen.

We'd spent much of the day running errands for Altovise, first rushing to Verizon, and then to Cingular Wireless, to get her cell phone problem resolved. Afterward, we headed to one of her banks. Altovise then asked me to stop at Value Self Storage on University

Parkway, so we could clear out her belongings. The rental company was next door to her old apartment complex. Now that she had the key, we'd organize and pack up all of her things, then ship most of them to her address in New York. Altovise planned to spend some time there, cleaning and restoring the two-family home her mother had left her.

As I drove toward the gate, Altovise realized that she didn't know the entrance code to open it. So, I parked the car and we went into the office. There, Altovise greeted two female employees. She inquired about the code, but, since she didn't know which storage room was hers, they asked for her identification. They checked, but couldn't find her name on the leasing contract.

"Are you Carol Francis?" asked one woman.

"No," Altovise replied.

Only Tony and his wife were listed on the leasing agreement, so Altovise was denied access to her own storage room. Stunned, she immediately tried to contact Tony, only to reach his voicemail. After a few minutes, she tried again. When they finally spoke – in what was an intense exchange – they arranged to meet at the facility later that day. I wasn't sure of what to expect, but, at least, we'd have some help moving the heavy things.

Later, about an hour before closing time, we returned to meet Tony. I pulled the car over so I wouldn't block the entrance. When he finally showed up, he gestured to me to park my car on the side while he turned toward the gate. Obviously, he wanted me to park my car in the lot.

"No!" Altovise stammered. "Go in!"

I put on the brakes and turned the car toward Tony's vehicle. Noticing this, he hit the brakes hard and his car jerked to a stop. Angrily, he pointed and insistently yelled, "Park over there!"

"No!" Altovise yelled. "Go in with him...follow him!"

I felt like an old Gumby toy, pulled from one leg and yanked from the other. Even worse, I was gripped with fear. The man's tone was threatening; he had an intensity that I felt, even from there.

"He wants us to park!" I shouted back, frustrated. "I'm not going to fight with him." No, I'd already seen how confrontational he was. Saturday's scene was still fresh in my memory. "He doesn't want...He's not going to let us in!"

It seemed too incredulous to be happening. Why was he blocking us? What on earth could be in there that was worth all this?

Somewhere in the back of my mind, I must have realized the irony of the situation. Back in 1991, during the financial turmoil following Sammy's death, the tax court ordered an auction of his possessions to pay their huge tax debt. Most observers were shocked by this development, believing it would never happen. But, it did. During the second of three auctions, Butterfield & Butterfield sold five hundred pieces of memorabilia, clothing, and jewelry, including Sammy's gold record for "The Candy Man." The sale netted approximately $439,000. In the other auctions, most of Sammy's gun collection, valuable paintings, and art were also sold.

Altovise was unsuccessful in her court plea to allow her to keep some of Sammy's things. So, apparently, she considered another course of action. Some months later, she was ordered to appear in court after it was determined that over 180 pieces of jewelry where missing from the list of items in their insurance inventory. Also, unaccounted for were five fur coats, a portrait of Sammy by LeRoy Neiman, and a valuable Campbell's Soup Can painting by the famous artist, Andy Warhol. It was believed that Altovise hid the items with the help of two others.

In a bizarre twist, many of the items actually turned up in a Burbank storage room. It was reportedly rented by one of Altovise's employees, but, somehow, the lease was executed with a stolen driver's license. The only reason it grabbed the attention of the authorities was because a rental bill of some $365, hadn't been paid. The manager of the facility had contacted the driver on the card, only to find that he wasn't involved. That's when the police were flagged. It's likely that the location of the items would never have been discovered had Altovise, or her employees, kept up with the payments

Years later, an attorney had successfully petitioned to have some of the items that were not auctioned, returned to her. I wondered about this. Were the returned items now locked in this storage room? Why did Tony seem determined to keep us from reaching them? Altovise was equally determined that he'd acquiesce and let us in.

In an apologetic tone, I said, "I can't force him! I don't even know him!" As my words sank in, she relented, and I slowly backed up and parked the car in the lot.

Tony, meanwhile, punched in the code and disappeared behind the gate.

Altovise and I proceeded to the office, where I spotted a side door leading to the storage grounds. Since it was unlocked, we quickly stepped outside and immediately spotted Tony's vehicle parked several feet away. We dashed over to the storage room as he was opening it up.

This was the first time I'd seen Tony up close, and I was surprised by his appearance.

For some reason, I'd expected an older looking man, though I didn't know why. His hair was curly and he had smooth brown skin much like Altovise's. He was a short, but attractive man, probably around Sammy's height, and I suddenly recalled having seen a professional photo of him back in Altovise's old apartment. It was like those used by actors.

Altovise marched right up to Tony, sparks flying, as the tension between them mounted. Tony immediately started shouting at Altovise, who didn't hesitate to defend herself. He had another key, and as he yelled at her, he dangled it above her head.

Demanding money, he said that she couldn't withdraw her things until she paid him.

"I've already paid you!" she yelled, incredulously. "I paid you!"

She reminded him that she'd just put $2,500 in his hand. Tony, however, wanted another $500.

"What?!" she yelled, completely aghast. "I'm not paying you another cent!"

Altovise was determined to hold her ground, but Tony wasn't budging, either. He started shouting about the expenses he'd paid for her, and that seemed to signal my exit cue. Their words were loud and bitter, and I was too uncomfortable to stay and hear them. So, I excused myself, although I doubt that either of them heard me. Back in the office, I tried to steady my hands, but I was shaking uncontrollably.

Moments later, Altovise reentered the office, apologizing for the ugly encounter. Calming herself, she asked me to come with her, because they'd worked out some agreement.

When we reached the rental unit, Tony was busy moving some of the boxes around. He'd cooled off considerably, and when we approached him, he tried to force a charming smile. Some residue of shock must have remained on my face. Slightly embarrassed, he made a vague attempt to introduce himself. I simply nodded. Altovise was dead silent.

Feeling some obligation, Tony began to explain his position. He wanted me to know that he and his wife had paid for the storage room. Now, they needed to be reimbursed. Glancing at Altovise he said, "She just left town without bothering to tie up the loose ends."

He seemed oblivious to the possibility that I'd known of Altovise's departure, the strange timing of her eviction, and the troubling questions that surrounded it. He failed to mention that she'd moved into Barrett's house, so I didn't mention that I, myself, had stayed there. In fact, I didn't make any reply. I allowed him to ramble on. Tony fumed over having to pack up all her things because "she wasn't responsible enough to come back and get them." Both, Altovise and I still remained silent.

I moved toward some of the boxes, but Tony quickly stopped me. He insisted on handling everything himself. He'd brought large boxes in which to pack all the smaller ones. Then, they'd be ready to ship to New York. However, we had to handle first things first.

"Get in," said Tony, opening the back door of his vehicle. "We don't have much time. We've got to get to the bank!"

Altovise had apparently agreed to his terms, so we needed to now get to her bank, or an ATM machine and rush back. We didn't have a moment to waste, and that was probably the strategy for waiting so long. Altovise was leaving the following morning, and this was her last chance to get her things, at least, on this trip. The hourglass was in motion, and this eleventh-hour pressure tactic worked well for Tony. During the uncomfortable moments that followed, he did all the driving and most of the talking.

"Why didn't you want to introduce me to your friend?" Tony chuckled, as he glanced at Altovise in the rearview mirror. She had opted to sit in the back seat with me, and didn't respond to his question. It was true that I hadn't been introduced on Saturday, but the reason was obvious enough. Just like on this occasion, the scene was very intense. Why would she have heightened it?

Despite the awkward situation, Altovise was surprisingly calm. In fact, when she finally spoke, the serenity in her voice made her seem strangely removed from it all. "Yes, Tony," she softly remarked. "You're right."

Tony must have detected a hint of sarcasm, though, and seemed intent on shaking her up. He began to berate her for running away without handling her affairs.

"You just left!" he shouted, "You left everything in a mess. There were the bills and the apartment and all your things."

All the while, Altovise silently nodded, as though in agreement. The calmer that she appeared, the angrier he became. "Your problem is, you don't love anyone," he said, glaring at her through the rearview mirror.

This struck me as odd. Why did he take the argument in that direction?

"You're right, Tony," she responded, almost numbly. "I don't love anyone."

"You didn't even see after your mother," he said accusingly.

My discomfort was reaching a whole new level. As we turned off of University Parkway, onto Honore, he finally pushed the button to unhinge her.

"Did you even see about her ashes?" he yelled. Before she could answer, he lashed out, "No! They're still at my house! You didn't even care enough to get your mother's ashes!"

He'd gone too far.

"Just send them to me, Tony!" she fired back. "Send me the ashes!"

At this point, I felt like leaping from the car. His words were so unnecessary. Why was he talking about such things in front of a total stranger? It was disrespectful to both of us and totally inappropriate.

Here I was, sitting in the car of a man whom I didn't know, trapped in the midst of argument that was out of control. I got so nervous, I started shaking again. I kept wondering why this was happening. Why was he trying to agitate her? This was emotional battery. I couldn't understand the purpose of this.

Altovise suddenly turned things around.

"Tony, where is the billfold?" she asked, pointedly.

"What?" he stuttered, off balance for the first time.

"Where is the Burton billfold?" she demanded. "And the ring. You know, I gave them to you to hold, and I want them back!"

Still stuttering, Tony now checked for my reaction in the mirror. His voice was much lower: "I don't think I have them, but I'll look in the garage. I'll look through some of that stuff and see if I find them."

"I'd appreciate that!" she snapped. Evidently, they'd had this discussion before, because she obviously felt Tony was holding out on her.

Altovise would later share the stories surrounding the two precious keepsakes. She was actually referring to the Presidential Ring which was given to Sammy years ago when they visited President Richard Nixon at The White House. That visit was historic, as well as controversial, and the ring always meant a great deal to Sammy.

According to Altovise, she and Tony were getting ready to meet friends for dinner at a restaurant, when he asked if he could wear the ring. She'd agreed, although she'd already given him one of Sammy's other rings as a gift. This one, however, was a special Presidential award which he could use only for that particular evening. Altovise said the ring was never returned.

Something else disappeared that night. In a generous gesture, Altovise had passed Tony a billfold with money to help pay for the dinner. She was once confused about the details, but certain about one point: she'd extended the billfold to Tony. Richard Burton had given the billfold to Sammy as a gift, and after Sammy's death, Altovise had given it to Richard's wife. Sometime later, his wife returned the gift to Altovise. Now, both, the Burton billfold and the Presidential Ring were gone.

There was a hush for a few moments. Tony turned into the bank parking lot, and I was thankful that we'd arrived at the ATM. It was a short trip, but it had felt like an eternity.

Altovise quietly opened the door and got out. Tony glanced at her as she passed, and wasted no time in briefing me on their history together. If I wasn't sufficiently shaken, he'd remove the last vestiges of comfort by initiating an impromptu inquisition.

"Are you related to Josh?" he inquired, fearful that I was.

"No," I responded.

"Do you know Josh?" he asked.

"No," I replied.

Honestly, I'd never met Josh. However, I did know who he was, and more importantly, that his father was Minister Louis Farrakhan. I recalled that Farrakhan had demanded that Tony return the items he'd taken from Altovise's safety deposit box. Understandably, Tony now felt threatened by him. I also recalled hearing something about Josh having relatives in Florida. That's probably why Tony was worried that I was one of them.

"Do you know Tracey?" he continued. "I think my wife must have met you, once," he said, fishing for answers. Now, it was clear that he was confusing me with Lisa, whom he'd apparently never met.

"No, I don't think I've met your wife," I replied. I was determined to avoid any discussions of Tracey.

"Alto tells all her friends these things about me, like I'm a bad person. She never tells them how her mother desperately pleaded with me to take care of her daughter. 'Baby boy,' she'd cry, Alto was laying on the floor, out of control, and her mother was crying, 'Please help her!' She never tells 'em about those times, and the money I've spent… and how I saved her life!"

My mouth was probably open, but I couldn't get any words out.

"She was with your friends? Was she out drinking?" he asked, studying my face through the mirror.

"No," I replied, defensively. "My friends. They…they're Christians," I stammered, as though Christians never drink.

Altovise was punching the keys at the ATM machine and looking frustrated.

"Look at her!" he exclaimed. "She's so drunk, she can't even figure out her code. Look at her!"

I knew this couldn't be true. I'd been with Altovise all day, running errands in the car. She'd had no opportunity to have a drink. We'd scarcely had time for lunch.

"Look at that! She's so confused, she can't even figure it out!" he shouted. I sat in silence trying to sort it out, myself. Why was he portraying her that way? She'd clearly had no opportunity to drink. However, I wondered why she couldn't get her money out. Was she so worked up, she couldn't concentrate?

Riled up and impatient, Tony finally jumped out of the car. He rushed to the machine, and without saying much to Altovise, started pushing in the code. Astonished, I watched as the scene progressed. How did he know her ATM code? I wondered.

Moments passed without success. Now, Tony also looked frustrated. I began to feel a deep sense of dread. Was the machine down? If they couldn't withdraw the funds, I feared he'd really explode.

Tony decided to try one of Altovise's other accounts. Finally, he hit the jackpot and they headed back to the car. I sat, totally stunned by what I'd witnessed. Later, somewhat vaguely, Altovise indicated that she'd already withdrawn her limit from the first account and hadn't enough funds available.

Back at the storage room, Tony quickly repackaged all of Altovise's things and loaded them up in his vehicle. I looked at the room wondering why he'd chosen to rent so much space. It seemed much too large for Altovise's possessions. Hadn't they all used this space at one time? Shouldn't they have been splitting the cost?

We quickly headed to the UPS Store, and within less than an hour, we were back. Altovise's things were officially on their way to New York. With the clearing of her belongings – her only remaining ties to Sarasota – the storage room drama had finally drawn to a close.

# 22

## COCKTAILS AND ROUND THREE

*Early August 2006*
*Sarasota, Florida*

ltovise kept apologizing for the unpleasant encounter with
Tony. She seemed genuinely shocked by his behavior, but
I knew it wasn't the first conflict they'd had. I surprised myself when I suggested that we pray for him. Altovise was momentarily
speechless and must have wondered if I was serious. I wondered, myself. To be honest, I wasn't really in a forgiving mood, no matter how
spiritual I felt.

However, something extraordinary began to occur. The episode
prompted Altovise to reexamine her business dealings with her partners, specifically regarding their commission structure. She'd called
Barrett to discuss the incident, and he'd agreed – at least, over the
phone – to modify their arrangement. They would ask their attorney
to draft a letter to Tony, officially cutting off his commissions on her
earnings.

"That's a wise move," I told her, wondering if our morning prayer
had released a miracle. I was puzzled, however, about the commission
structure, because, at the time, I didn't know the details.

"Well, Tony introduced me to Barrett," she explained. "So, he gets
a commission for all of that. Since I've been with Barrett, things have
gotten better. He's found money for me; tracked down people who

claimed they couldn't find me. He works real hard and he's made a real difference."

"So, what does Tony get?" I asked.

"Ten percent of what I get."

"And what's Barrett's commission?" I inquired.

"Twenty percent," she responded.

Trying not to look horrified, I nodded. "Yeah, I think you're taking the right step."

Altovise looked rejuvenated that night as she awaited a call from her escort for the evening. I vaguely remember that her friend's name was Carl Mazu. He was a deep sea explorer who'd long retired from all his voyages. She mentioned that he'd actually once sailed with the famous explorer Jacques Cousteau. When he called for directions, though, he decided against navigating through any new waters. He was fearful that he might get lost trying to find us. Instead, he suggested I phone for a cab. Altovise would meet him at Bacco's, an Italian restaurant that was then located in downtown Sarasota.

"Bacco's?" I whispered, trying to envision the place. The cabdriver, of course, was familiar with the spot, and as I waved goodbye, I hoped that Altovise would have a good time.

A friend and her daughter were visiting when Altovise phoned a few hours later. Her voice was gleeful and lighthearted, so was Carl's when he took the phone. Being well fortified, he was ready to venture to my home. When I inquired about how the evening was going, he laughed, "Alto's trying to get me drunk!"

Whether or not this was true, his sparkling red Mercedes pulled into our driveway a short time later, and they were as giddy as two carousing sailors. I was sure I'd never seen Altovise as resplendent as she appeared. Carl smiled with the same dazzling quality with which his car glimmered in the moonlight. As he waved goodbye, I remember thinking that he seemed to possess a very special quality.

Altovise floated into the house much like a teenager coming home from a date. I didn't have to ask if she'd had a good time. That much was obvious.

Inside, she took a seat on the living room couch. Beside her was my friend, Renessa, who was passionately discussing the nature of her spirituality. This didn't seem to shake Altovise's euphoric spirit, and she sat, looking enthralled by Renessa's words. Although it was getting late, no one seemed ready to retire, as the atmosphere was cozy and we'd started talking about relationships. Altovise, who was curled up with her legs beneath her, seemed delighted to have this time to talk. She began to reminisce about some of her fondest memories, like those she recalled from Washington D.C.

"You know, Sammy and I were the first Black Americans to overnight at the White House as guests," she told us.

"Wow," I murmured, considering the historic significance. I realized how proud she felt about this.

My mother had entered the room, and was now seated in a chair on the other side of the room. She was obviously interested in our discussion, but with one particular thought in mind – politics, to be precise. She was a devout Democrat, and at that moment, she was mulling over a hot issue that was steaming up the political arena.

It was a campaign year and with only a few months before the election, mom couldn't resist bringing up her views, especially concerning Democrats and Republicans. She started questioning each guest with regard to something President Bush had done.

Apparently, this sparked some unpleasant memories for Altovise and her mood began to sour. Her body language indicated an immediate sense of danger and she suddenly straightened up. It was unmistakable. I felt it, too. We were drifting toward a hazardous area.

"Well, let's not get into all that," I said, chuckling. I tried to shift our discussion back to something innocuous. Mom, however, was insistent. She went on to imply that anyone in their right mind would never support a Republican.

Oops, I thought, sensing the need for damage control. Altovise looked uncomfortable. Her high had suddenly leveled off. Mom seemed to be baiting her in an attempt to get a declaration of her affiliation. I'd never known about Altovise's political views, and now, as her eyes began to glare, I knew it wasn't the right time to find out.

"People can support whomever they want!" she snapped, her voice elevated with anger.

I had to stop this conversation, as things were about to become explosive.

"Mom," I whispered, "Let's not get into politics, tonight."

It was too late, however. Mom always loved a good argument, and the powerful components were already present. "I'm just saying that it doesn't make sense," Mom said. "Who could even support these people?"

Altovise, now fully stirred, moved to the edge of the couch as though she'd leap off. She was nearly sneering at mom. She'd gone back to memories of Sammy's controversial support of the Republican Party.

"You know, it was so unfair of people to criticize Sammy the way that they did, just for going to the convention. It really hurt him," she said. Altovise was referring to the infamous moment when Sammy made the headlines for hugging President Nixon at the Republican convention. The public outcry over this affair, especially from out-raged Afro-Americans, would leave Sammy with a deep wound. Now, seeing Altovise's pained expression, I knew that it was still very sensi-tive turf.

The timing of this conversation couldn't have been worse. Altovise was still upset over Sammy's missing Presidential Ring. She told me that there had been cufflinks that matched it. The Ring was one of the last keepsakes she had from their White House visit, or, at least, the most treasured one. Understandably, she was more sensitive than ever about any criticism directed toward this experience.

I tried to steer the conversation toward a safer topic, but didn't suc-ceed. My mother voiced another critical opinion of Republican sup-porters, and the tension in the air became so thick it nearly choked me. As I cleared my throat, I heard Altovise sneer: "Everyone's en-titled to support who they want to!"

Then, following an awkward silence, she abruptly stood up and stormed out of the room. Everyone's mouth hung open, and after a few moments, Renessa finally commented: "She was really upset!"

"Think so?" I replied.

# 23

## THE MORNING AFTER

*Early August 2006*
*Sarasota, Florida*

I was relieved to see Altovise back in good spirits the following morning. I was preparing breakfast when I spotted her coming toward the kitchen and inquired about the restaurant where she'd had dinner.

"Was it nice?" I asked, slicing a mango.

"Oh, yes," she replied. "The owner came over and talked with us a long time. I told him about our project, and he says we can use the restaurant for a fundraiser."

"Really?" I said, as surprised by her actions as I was by his offer.

"You should go by there," she continued, "And take a look. Introduce yourself."

"Yeah," I replied. "I will."

Altovise gave me the owner's business card and told me that he expected to hear from us.

My heart was pounding at the thought. It sounded too good to be true. Was this really Altovise talking? Was she finally getting behind our project with something more than sweet words of encouragement?

When my mother once asked Altovise why she'd moved back to L.A., she'd replied, "It's better for your daughter that I'm there. It's better for our screenplay, because that's where all my contacts are."

However, the weeks had passed, and then the months, and now a whole year seemed to have been lost because we'd made no progress.

With no offers, I knew it was time for us to brainstorm. We needed to figure out where we were headed. We'd already entertained the idea of writing the book version of our story.

The other consideration was to produce it independently.

"Could we actually do it?" I'd asked. "Why not?" I responded, answering my own question.

I felt encouraged, knowing that Spike Lee had made his first film, *She's Gotta' Have It,* with a modest budget. Robert Rodriquez took his camera and a friend across the Mexican border, and with only $7,000, shot *El Mariachi*, another successful movie. We, too, could go to Mexico, where it was cheaper to shoot, lodge, and handle the logistics.

"We can do this," Altovise agreed. "We can make this film."

Sammy had made movies, and formed his own production company to create them. Altovise was a trained actress and even starred in a few films, though Sammy joked about their merit. Still, she'd acquired some real film-making experience and appeared in shows like *Charlie's Angels*, so she knew something about the process. Most importantly, she knew some very heavy hitters in Hollywood. All we had to do was get the ball in motion. We had the most important assets: a great story and script. If we got the financing, we could film our movie the way that we'd envisioned it.

Altovise was thrilled by the prospect of being the executive producer of her own film. In fact, she said that she'd already assumed this role in a future biopic about Sammy's life, as well as a documentary, still on the table.

"I could even star in it myself!" she added.

I realized that Altovise was more excited about producing the film than actually selling it. I wanted to pinch myself. Why had I missed this? During that past year, she'd been so consumed by her problems that it was difficult to gauge her true feelings. Depression had been a major factor, as well as a sense of defeat and powerlessness.

Now, Altovise was like a completely new woman. I thought about this as I finished the fruit salad.

"You seem so much better, Alto," I said. "You're so much more alive and full of energy."

She smiled and shared part of the reason. First, she said, an Applebee's commercial featuring Sammy had been helpful, financially. She also relished the new activities in her life, especially back in New York. She was repairing and cleaning the property she'd inherited from her mother. This gave her a bi-coastal lifestyle in which she spent several weeks working on the house in Queens and several weeks back in L.A.

"What do you think I should do with the house?" she asked me. "My friends say I should sell it."

"No!" I exclaimed. "You have to have a safety net. You should always have your own property, in case anything happens."

Altovise listened closely as I explained: "Look, you've got a property. Unless something unusual happens, it always goes up in value."

She appreciated my advice because I'd once been a realtor, and I convinced her that it was more pragmatic to keep and improve the property than to simply get rid of it.

"That money you get could be gone in a year," I warned. "Keep the property and make it work for you."

So, Altovise continued to work on the house. Since it was a two-family structure, she decided to rent out part of it, and use the other for herself.

"Which unit do you think I could live in?" she'd asked.

"I haven't seen it, so I can't tell you. But, pick the one that you like best for yourself."

I was amazed, that day, as I looked at Altovise. She seemed to have a new sense of power, and she was now determined to bring our story to the screen.

"We can do this," I whispered to myself. "We can do this thing."

Altovise, who was gung-ho, said, "Yes, we can do this!"

As I drove her to the airport, we talked about potential financiers, actors, and actresses. Art had suggested someone like Bow Wow for one of the roles, and we already knew that Geoffrey Owens was on board.

Sandra, smiling happily in the back seat, sensed that we were on another adventure. She'd formed a close bond with Altovise, who – during her short visit – insisted on helping shop for Sandra's new school supplies. In my daughter's mind, we were still the Three Musketeers, stumbling from one escapade to another.

Now, Altovise was heading back to New York, but we still had a great deal of work ahead of us. Promising to call when she arrived, she cheerfully waved as she left the car. As I waved back, I still couldn't get over how great she looked.

Later that night, Altovise left a message on my voicemail, apologizing, again, for the ugly encounter with Tony, but thanking me for having her at my home. From the tone of her voice, she was thoroughly excited about the work ahead of us.

I called Altovise, a couple of days later, after hearing about a terrorist attack in Europe. I urged her to be careful when making any travel plans, and if she was heading back toward the West Coast, consider waiting until it was safer. Heeding this advice, she extended her stay.

As it turned out, Altovise would spend many of the following months in Queens. She said that her son, Manny, had come home from the service. He'd settled in New York, where he could now check on her. Altovise mentioned that she was trying to help him find a job.

"What type of career does he want?" I asked.

"I'm not really sure," she replied. "But he loves to play the piano."

That season, the two would travel up to Foxwoods Casino, in Connecticut, to see a show devoted to Sammy's music. Altovise said they had a wonderful time.

She was also thrilled about plans in the works to have a statue built in Sammy's likeness. Altovise said she'd meet with U.S. Congressman Charles Rangel to discuss the possibility of designating a spot for it in New York. From her description, it would be huge, and I couldn't wait to see it.

There were arrangements underway, as well, to have Sammy's star placed in Las Vegas. In fact, Altovise was looking forward to traveling to several new venues to promote Sammy's legacy.

In the meantime, she had some promising news about the house she was repairing. There was a potential tenant who was interested in renting part of it. Altovise said the woman was a teacher, and that she wanted to get everything in order.

# 24

## UNSOLVED MYSTERY: CHEETAH OR CHEATER GIRLS?

*September 2006*
*Sarasota, Florida*

During the weekend of September 25, 2006, a situation occurred which posed a crisis beyond anything I'd ever expected. While sitting at home that Saturday night, watching a made-for-television movie, it dawned on me that it was strange to be viewing it alone. Sandra had watched the premiere of the Disney film the previous night and wasn't interested in seeing it again. For some reason she also didn't have a desire to take me up on an offer to go out for ice cream. Was she coming down with a fever? I'd cancelled a date, just so I could spend some time with her, and here I sat watching a kids' program all alone in our family room. Maybe we both were coming down with something.

Raven Symone starred in the feature, the actress whom I'd considered for our film. In fact, it seemed like the perfect marriage – our musical, and her talent – and since Michael had been a writer and supervising producer on her show, we had someone to pitch the idea to her. Altovise, however, still felt she was unsuitable for the role.

The promotional blitz for Disney's ***The Cheetah Girls 2: When In Spain*** created a huge buzz, particularly among thousands of young girls. All across the country, they exhibited something close to hysteria just prior to its broadcast. It was the sequel to the first *Cheetah Girls* film, a Disney product that included a book series by the same name. The stories followed the escapades of a singing group made up of four teenage girls. The first film's popularity, and the phenomenal success of *High School Musical,* had proven that musicals were not only viable, but extremely profitable. In fact, that's why Michael said it was an ideal time to sell our screenplay. The company was actively scouting for musicals.

As the date of the premier drew closer, the anticipation of *The Cheetah Girls* film soared.

Sandra, being a big fan of Raven's, found the excitement to be contagious. Caught up in the media hoopla, like many of her class-mates, she'd planned to host a "Cheetah Girls Party." That Friday, although only one friend actually attended, they'd gorged on pizzas and celebrated the occasion as though it were an official holiday. Not surprisingly, it wasn't an isolated affair. As far as viewers, the film would break numerous records. In fact, it would be broadcast several times, at least once in Spanish, and during that season, its unprec-edented ratings made it the highest viewed, original, made-for-televi-sion Disney movie.

I wouldn't be able to appreciate the ratings, though, not that Saturday night, nor any nights to follow, because I was distracted by something else. The film's plot was strangely familiar to me. There was an uncanny, almost eerie resemblance between this film's theme and ours. Even the unique twists in their story seemed remarkably similar to those in *A Detour to Mexico,* only the location and the char-acters were different.

Initially, I felt somewhat flattered by a few of the similarities. It gave credence to my feelings that we had a hit story. Halfway through, however, I began to feel uneasy. Although the subplots differed, I spotted too many elements that I recognized. I felt confused, then alarmed. Red flags were flying everywhere. What was I witnessing? Was I just imagining it, or was this our story?

"No!" I shouted. "It can't be!"

I looked more closely. There were obvious differences. ***The Cheetah Girls 2: When in Spain*** film focused on four teenage girls as opposed to four members of a family, and they performed in Spain instead of Mexico. Still, there were scenes and relationships that I knew in the intimate way in which a mother knows her own children.

"No," I whispered, again. "I've just been working too hard."

Still, I recognized my own characters and these seemed just like them, only thinly camouflaged to fit the needs of this sequel. I thought of Kimberly, Alex, and all the other main players and began to replay all the things they did. I'd spent many days and nights creating their individual personalities, motives, and dialogue. I'd planned their every action as I moved them from scene to scene. Through eleven rewrites of 117 pages, I'd practically lived with them, editing the material until it rang with authenticity. Now, it felt as though I'd given our characters the breath of life only to release them to a cruel and treacherous world.

What had I done? A horrifying feeling overcame me. I began to cross-examine myself.

What was the likelihood that it really happened? How could it have happened, anyway?

I paced around the room, struggling to make sense of it. Maybe I was paranoid and simply hallucinating. It couldn't really be what I was thinking. After all, I'd taken steps to protect our story. I'd applied for the copyright and registered it with the Writers Guild West. That information was right on the cover of all of our materials. Who would dare to take it?

Admittedly, I wasn't feeling very spiritual at that moment. If anything, it felt as though my faith was shaken. In fact, my whole world was shaken. What on earth was happening? I desperately needed an explanation, some way to cope with my confusion. Was there something wrong with me? Or, did I really see what I thought I saw? My breathing became strained. I was hyperventilating, like someone confronted by a rattlesnake.

The reality sank in and I began to panic. I was an unknown, powerless writer, with no big guns behind me. Overwhelmed with fear, I began to cry. I tried to comfort myself, but I felt a deep sense of hopelessness. One moment I wanted to contact the media, but in the next, I was too scared to utter a sound. I'd never known this type of fear.

"God, help me!" I cried.

I managed to get to church the next day, but I couldn't lift my voice in song. I'd barely slept and I was exhausted. I'd come there only for answers, but I went home feeling empty.

That night, armed with a pad and pen, I camped out in the same position and watched the third showing of the film. I wrote notes about each scene, so I could more carefully compare the two plots. New things caught my eye. Although there were obvious differences in the sub-plots, there were areas that nearly mimicked our screenplay. The fact that the main scenarios were nearly identical didn't bother me; an international talent competition was too common to be unique. I didn't even worry about both settings taking place in a Spanish-speaking country. However, the other similarities disturbed me.

I'd added several unique features to *A Detour to Mexico* to give it a special feeling. Incredibly, these elements were also in the film. I tried to overlook a few of them. For example, the fact that, in both stories there was a beach party held for the contestants, and it was during this scene that a romantic liaison ignited. I decided to ignore it, especially since there were so many other strange coincidences.

One of the most stunning parallels was the early use of a magical, somewhat otherworldly, occurrence, which, in both cases, took place at the bedroom window of the main character. What was most striking was how both stories had this pivotal, supernatural moment in which a teenage girl – the main singer and composer in each case – made a seemingly 'impossible wish.' This request would reveal not only her deepest feelings about life – and the key message in her songs – but establish the main theme of each story. It would be difficult to miss the significance because, in both plots, it was this moment that launched a musical journey in which the request, itself, would be miraculously answered. It was fulfilled, however, only after each group experienced the trials that led to the culminating scenes and the dramatic conclusion.

Most amazing, however, was the presence in both stories of a special Spanish guitarist with a very special purpose. In both cases, he'd meet the main characters in an open-air restaurant, serenading them while they were eating. In both stories, the visiting group was amazed by his romantic music, and the love that he expressed for his land. As in our own screenplay, this unique 'angel' played his guitar so passionately that he touched and bedazzled everyone who heard him. It was this enchanting, omnipresent character who would secretly witness what no one else saw – a disastrous problem that threatened to disrupt the group's performance. In both plots, it was the knowledge that he held, and the manner in which he acted on it, that would ultimately determine the outcome of the story. Not only did this youth save the day for each group, but he would change their lives in a meaningful way. Unless I was mistaken, I was viewing an older version of Miguel, the young Mexican guitarist whom we'd created in Barnes & Noble.

There were other striking parallels, especially in recalling the first version of our screenplay. In each plot an inner conflict developed within the main singing group, a rift that would trigger a crisis just days before their scheduled performance. In both stories, this inner fighting would be exploited by the group's greatest adversary. I was stunned by the identical manner in which one character, in particular, maneuvered. The mother/manager of the group's main competitor initially approached them with sweet smiles and helpful gestures. This character would try to use her daughter to further divide the group. In *A Detour to Mexico,* it was the mother/daughter combination of Lilian and Marci. In *The Cheetah Girls 2,* it was the mother/daughter combination of Lola and Marisol. In each case, the daughter befriended the most rebellious member of the group – the one who wanted to replace the group's signature style with their own. It was a clever effort to further divide, destabilize, and sabotage their performance. Channel wanted to replace Galleria's song about friendship with a Spanish piece. Alex wanted to replace Kimberly's song about love with a hip-hop piece. In both situations, the mutiny would pose a threat to the group's unity. When this failed to defeat them, the calculating mother would resort to more drastic measures. In both cases, she bragged about her knowledge of the area, made suggestions about where to go, and gave advice that ultimately led to trouble.

In both stories, the group's inner rivalry posed a major challenge to the composer, her style, and her message. While the clock was ticking, the singer/composer had to overcome a personal crisis brought on by self-doubt. She'd lost faith in her own message. The real question revolved around her belief in the truth in her music and her ability to pull things back together in time to compete.

In *A Detour to Mexico,* Kimberly's lyrics were about unfailing love, and throughout the story, her belief in love would be tested. In *The Cheetah Girls 2: When in Spain,* Galleria's lyrics were about unfailing friendship, and throughout the story, her belief in friendship would be tested.

Would Kimberly's belief in love prevail? Would she be able to perform her song about love?

Would Galleria's belief in friendship prevail? Would she be able to perform her song about friendship?

In both cases, the answer came only after they stepped on stage. Remarkably, at that climatic moment, it was the Spanish guitarist who would set the stage when he struck the first notes of the singer's own music with his guitar. Incredible as it seemed, even the ending was much the same.

The situation reminded me of a bakery shop where I'd once considered buying two different cakes. One was covered with shredded coconut, the other topped with bits of candy. I knew, however, that if I removed all the topping from each one, I'd find they were made from the same batter, which meant they came from the very same source.

When the film was over, I sat virtually paralyzed. Drained. Everything in my life seemed to shut down for a few days. All I could think of was the tremendous amount of work that had gone completely to waste, and the loss of all of our dreams. I'd put everything I had into our screenplay, from the research and writing, to the editing and re-writing. Then, there were all the letters I'd sent. I kept thinking about the stressful trip to the West Coast and the meeting in Beverly Hills.

Was it only meant to be an introductory exercise, an initiation into Hollywood for the unschooled and unprotected? Where was our agent? Was there no one to represent us? Did we have no rights at all?

Altovise went silent when I first called her. For the longest time, I couldn't make her understand what had happened. I knew she'd heard my words, but she didn't seem to be processing them.

"I'm sorry," I said, feeling guilty about letting her down. "I really thought I'd protected it."

During the following days, I tried to retrace my actions and remember everything that had happened. Who had actually seen our materials? I'd written several people, but very few actually received hard copies of our screenplay. I didn't feel comfortable with the thoughts that now came to mind. Still, I wasn't in a position to dismiss them. Other than Altovise, there were only three people whom I'd given hard copies of our materials: Michael, Geoffrey, and Art.

Maybe I was paranoid, but the more I looked at the situation, the more startling it appeared, because there were more coincidences than just those found in the stories. What was alarming was a frightening set of circumstances that prompted a question that I wasn't even willing to address. I'd initially given the first version of our outline and materials to Michael. He worked closely with the very actress I'd envisioned for our film – Raven Symone. Oddly enough, she'd not only starred in the *Cheetah Girls* movie, but she'd also been one of the Executive Producers of the project. Then, there was the fact that the movie actually came out before the **Cheetah Girls** book by the same name, so it wasn't derived from the storybook.

New questions began to surface. An article I read suggested that the taping of **That's So Raven** ended because Raven went to Spain to do the film. Why did the sequence of developments seem so strange, and the planning so sudden?

More questions crept up and they sprouted much closer to home. I never doubted that Michael was a good guy. I'd always had full confidence in him. He'd always supported and encouraged me, and I knew he only wanted to help us get our screenplay produced. Yet, a horrible feeling overtook me, and increasingly, I felt torn inside. While I knew that he'd never do anything to harm me, I wondered if, in trying to garner interest in our project, he'd inadvertently exposed it to the wrong person.

Or had Art Rutter sent it to someone who borrowed part of it?

I called our agent that following week and shared my concerns about the film. Art stuttered a bit as he tried to comfort me and mentioned that it was possible that the producers may have used some of our material. He said they may have "retrofitted" it for **The Cheetah Girls** sequel. He assured me that he'd look into it, check out his files to see whom he'd sent it to, and give Michael a call. Art mentioned that Michael had a meeting the following day in which he was pitching a new idea, but that he'd talk with him afterwards. Art promised that he'd call me back within two days.

It would be the last time that we'd speak. To date, he's never called me back.

I called Michael, myself, and left a message at his house. Although I tried to steady my voice, I'm sure he heard the fear in my tone. In the message, I mentioned that something had gone wrong and I needed to speak with him. However, he didn't call back, not even to ask about the 'gigolo' project on which we were collaborating. I'd eventually receive a generic e-mail he sent to update numerous friends and acquaintances about his new show, **Cory In The House,** but when I called his number, once more, I wouldn't reach him.

About a year later, I'd open an e-mail from Michael in which he asked how the 'gigolo' project had gone. I didn't respond.

Geoffrey was the only other person who'd received the initial version of our screenplay. I phoned and left a message on his voicemail and about a week or so later he contacted me. He apologized for the delay. His father, U.S. Congressman Major Owens, was retiring and his brother was campaigning to fill his father's seat. Geoffrey had been in New York, trying to help out.

I quickly told him what had happened and asked if he'd spoken with anyone about our story. Geoffrey assured me that he hadn't spoken about it and definitely hadn't shown it to anyone. Frankly, he wasn't even sure where the script was, but he was certainly going to look for it.

Ironically, he'd had a role in one of the last episodes of **That's So Raven** and he was supposed to become a regular on the show, but it was suddenly cancelled, or something. He was in the dark as to why it ended so abruptly. It obviously caught him off guard.

There was one thing he felt fairly certain about; based on my description of **The Cheetah Girls** movie, he agreed that there were too many coincidences to be coincidental.

"Pam," he added. "Whoever used it had a hard copy of your screenplay. There're too many similarities for it to be from just word of mouth. Someone had it right in front of them."

I told Geoffrey that I'd let him know if I learned anything more.

I called Dave, hoping he could provide some legal advice or guide me to someone who could help. Like my other friends, he urged me to take action. Everyone was stressing the same message: "Don't just wimp away. Fight for what's yours."

I sighed, knowing it was easy for them to say. They weren't facing a mammoth giant like Disney. How would I fight without any money, especially against Disney's powerful legal division?

I called Altovise.

"I could contact Aaron Spelling's office," she mentioned. "But he just died, you know."

"Alto," I said. "We don't have anything left to produce. We'd have to re-write at least fifty percent of our story and somehow replace the most important parts."

That meant creating a completely different outcome. Even the main characters would have to undergo serious "surgery." I just wasn't up to it. I couldn't even image it.

"We could contact Spelling's assistant," she continued.

"No," I replied, "It's too late for that. We're going to have to fight this thing."

I wasn't sure if she could handle a lawsuit. It was all so ugly and frightening. I wasn't even sure that I was up to it. Actually, it seemed easier to pretend it never happened.

"We have to get an attorney," I told her. "My friend, Dave, mentioned one that may be able to help us."

Altovise was very quiet for a while, but she agreed that we had to take action.

I also started researching various law firms in California, looking for companies that handled intellectual property issues. In reading information listed on their Web sites, I was amazed by the number of firms that had client relationships with the Disney Corporation. I began to realize how colossal the company really was and how ant-like I felt in comparison.

During another conversation with Altovise, she made a suggestion. "If you don't mind," she began. "I'd like you to consider using my attorney."

"Sure," I responded. "What's his name?"

"Londell McMillan," she replied.

I smiled, because I'd just heard about him from another friend in Los Angeles who'd recommended him highly. My only concern was whether he represented Altovise or the partnership consisting of Altovise, Barrett and Tony. I asked her about this. Altovise advised me that the two men had introduced her to McMillan and that he represented all of them.

"Oh," I said. I had some initial reservations. After all, most of the attorney's dealings were probably through her managers, and that made me uncomfortable. However, out of respect for Altovise's wishes, and because he already represented her interests, I agreed to contact him.

I sent a formal letter requesting his legal guidance and representation. I followed up by phoning his office, where I reached one of his assistants. She requested that I forward to them more information about our screenplay, as well as *The Cheetah Girls* movie. I drafted a detailed description of the stories, and provided information chronicling the events that had taken place. Then I waited to hear from him.

After some time had passed, I called the office and was told that, since Attorney McMillan represented Altovise, he'd only be able to speak with her. She could reach him when he returned to the office after 2:00 p.m. I called Altovise and asked her to phone him. She hesitated, but said she would.

"Great," I replied. "Call me after you talk to him."

A day or two later, when I hadn't heard back from her, I called. "Did you reach him?" I asked, thankful that she was still in New York and near his East Coast office.

"No," Altovise replied. "I was cleaning out the garage."

She said she'd call him later that week.

A week passed, and when I called, she still hadn't contacted him.

"Why don't you phone him?" she asked me. "Then, we can do a three-way call."

I began to appreciate how awkward it was for Altovise, trying to speak about our screenplay. Although she'd helped create the characters, she hadn't actually written the story and she'd forgotten many of the details. She also hadn't seen the Disney movie and didn't carry the Disney Channel. We had a dilemma. The attorney would only speak to Altovise and I couldn't arrange to do a three-way.

"If you can call Mr. McMillan's office, then he can arrange to connect me," I suggested. She still hesitated. So, to boost her confidence, I faxed to her a summary of the two plots. When this was insufficient, I sent a very graphic outline to help her visualize and compare the similarities in each story. From these initial materials, I'd eventually write an eighty-six-page document about the stories.

The weeks passed, however, and nothing happened. Each time I spoke with Altovise, she gave another excuse for avoiding the attorney. More time passed and I began to feel anxious. Altovise's behavior was getting stranger and I couldn't figure out what was going on. I began to consider desperate measures, actions that were once unimaginable. I was frustrated enough to ask Altovise's managers for assistance.

"Perhaps you should alert Barrett," I finally suggested. "Maybe he can help us."

After a brief silence, Altovise agreed, but said he was on the West Coast and it was too early in the day to contact him. She'd call later when he was up.

Days passed.

The next time I spoke with Altovise, I raised the subject again, thinking I should call Barrett myself. This time, she said he was in London, but would be stopping in New York on his way back. That would be a good time to speak with him. Would I send another copy of the material for him to examine? I assured her that I would, and I rushed to the nearest Federal Express office to send another copy.

The following week I called to see if they'd had a chance to go over the letter and talk about the screenplay.

Altovise seemed confused. "What material?" she asked.

"Didn't Barrett come from London?" I asked.

"No," she replied. "He's in Los Angeles."

"But...but..." I stammered. For a moment, I couldn't speak at all. I suddenly felt breathless. "I'll call you back later," I uttered when, finally, I got my wind back.

I felt nauseated, like a child who'd spun around too long. The ground seemed to be spinning beneath me.

"No! No! No!" I cried. "This can't be happening!"

Immediately, I called Lisa, whom I hadn't spoken to in months.

"Lisa!" I said, when she answered. "I have to talk with you! It's an emergency and I need you to tell me the truth!"

"Girl, what's wrong!" she asked, terrified by my tone.

I told her everything that had happened, and how confused and frustrated I felt.

"Can you tell me what's going on?" I asked.

There was a long, dreadful silence on the phone. During those painful moments, I'd begin to reflect on the events that had transpired since the day we'd all had lunch. Lisa would eventually respond. However, somehow, I already knew the answer.

The events that took place over the following months would provide little comfort. In fact, while trying to find out what had happened to our screenplay, I'd discover more than I was prepared to handle. My eyes would be opened to a disturbing situation, the early evidence of which I'd completely ignored.

In early November, I went to a jazz concert in Lakewood Ranch where the talented musician, Marian Meadows, was performing. It was an outdoor event, and while walking around I ran into Tony Francis, who was sitting near the stage. I paused for a moment. Then, I realized that he might offer the only opportunity for me to get any answers. So, I walked up to him and reintroduced myself. He was cordial and seemed genuinely surprised when I explained that I'd tried to contact their lawyer. Tony seemed to be completely in the dark, at least about our screenplay. He promised, however, to contact McMillan and let me know what was going on.

About a week or so later, after he'd spoken with their attorney, Tony called to let me know what their attorney had decided. In his opinion, our evidence wasn't strong enough to win a case. Tony said that McMillan had already shared this with Altovise.

I was stunned. Why hadn't he or Altovise simply told me? I began to doubt the truthfulness of his words. After all, I'd always been wary of him.

Tony, however, didn't stop there. Much like the day when we'd met at the storage room, he had a great deal to say. He began, what would represent, part two of his history lesson about Altovise.

Complaining that she never appreciated him, he spoke at length about how he'd saved her life. He suggested that she wouldn't even be alive had it not been for his care, and he told me that he and Altovise's mother had split the bill for her last stay in a rehabilitation program. He claimed that he'd paid a sum that amounted to $15,000.

"Do you know," he exclaimed, "that I once got a check… and gave Alto about $15,000 and she went and bought a dress for about half that, and the dress is still in the bag it came in!"

He went on.

"You know, she tells people all these bad things about me, but not what happened when she was in the airport and wouldn't let us check what was in her bags, and there were all these water bottles filled with vodka. No, she doesn't tell people how we drained every one of those bottles. Or, did she tell you about how she got so sick onboard the plane and that we had to get her to a hospital? Did you know that?"

I didn't have a chance to answer.

"She has an old friend who's a physician," he continued, nearly rambling. "And she's even told us about Alto's problem."

"What do you mean?" I asked.

"Don't get me wrong. I know people feel that I could, but I've not gotten to the point where I'd have her declared to be mentally unfit, but…"

I held my breath.

"She's been drinking for years and her liver is damaged. Did you know she has cirrhosis of the liver? She's not supposed to drink a drop… not a drop! And she just won't stop!

"Yes," I replied. "I've known about the drinking."

Tony went on about the various things that Altovise had done throughout the years and how she'd enjoyed a wealthy and privileged lifestyle. "She's had her good times, and she's had furs and jewelry."

I stopped him at this point.

"What about her things," I began. "In her safety deposit box here?"

Much to my surprise, Tony wasn't the least bit embarrassed about the incident and talked opening, almost incessantly, about the things he'd taken.

"Those things?" he snickered. "They weren't even that valuable. The real valuable ones were sold and gone a long time ago. But I did bring them back."

"You brought all of them back?" I asked.

"Yeah," he said. "She had that Josh over there and that girl… Tracey, and they called his father and all. I brought all that stuff and put it back."

Tony went on to warn me that I couldn't trust Altovise. He said that she'd prove to be unfaithful in her friendship and wouldn't live up to any commitments.

"That's the way she is," he insisted. "She's never consistent."

He went on to say that he was tired of being her manager and that this would be his last year. Then he laughed and said he could make real money selling his story about what he'd experienced.

"You know, Alto's real problem," he said, suddenly sounding serious. "Her memory's shot. She has alcohol-induced dementia. Even her friend said this, and she's a doctor."

"What?" I asked.

"Yeah," he said, stressing again how he'd protected her. He'd put off the decision for quite some time to have her declared to be mentally unfit.

I suddenly felt dizzy, like I was getting nauseous. Knowing that I'd heard too much, it was time to hang up. I managed to thank Tony for looking into the matter for me and I said goodbye.

My thoughts raced back to various memories, particularly of things I couldn't quite understand. Then, I recalled Lisa telling me in our last conversation, "Pam, you're in denial."

I decided to call Altovise and share some of the things that Tony had said, warning her that he was telling friends that she suffered from dementia. While she never denied that she had "a memory problem," or an addiction to alcohol, she said, "People should help someone with this problem, not take advantage of them."

I copied the eighty-six page summary of the comparisons between the stories and sent them to a few attorneys closer to home. Lawyers in Florida shared a similar opinion that there were striking similarities between the two plots, and the question of probable access was undeniable, but even with strong evidence that suggested that our material was used, they couldn't be sure that we'd prevail. Since I had no money to cover a lengthy litigation, the firms would only take the case on a contingency basis if they were sure that it was unbeatable. After all, companies like Disney had their own attorneys and they were well experienced in this area. I was chasing a tiger in its own jungle.

One attorney took time to further explain that, an interpretation of the law actually allowed companies to use some parts of a writer's materials. Furthermore, in states like Florida, a judge would first preside over the case, not a jury, and he, or she, would follow criteria that favored the company in reaching a decision. It was the attorney's opinion that, if my case was tried before a jury, a group of my peers would probably rule in my favor. However, the law wouldn't play out that way. I heard her message loud and clear. I was small, poor and powerless, so the law wouldn't protect me.

As far as I was concerned, the verdict was already in and I was sentenced to a life of silence. Being forbidden to speak up was the ultimate ghostwriter's experience. I was present and, yet, invisible. The real irony was that I'd met Altovise with the objective of becoming her ghostwriter and I may have ended up being one of Disney's.

"Mom, where is God?" my daughter asked.

"He's right here with us," I replied. "We're just being tested."

Still, I would pray more than once about this and ask God for some type of explanation. Certainly, there were lessons that I could live without learning, and I found myself asking an old, familiar question: "Why me?"

I began to feel a twinge of guilt. Maybe, my inability to live a completely holy life had caused me to fail. Maybe this was my punishment for backsliding. I'd fallen from grace. What other explanation could there be?

Week after week, I sat on my lanai, trying to sort things out. My faith should have sustained me, but I was filled with self-pity. I managed to get to church, and during the ordeal, went to my pastor for counseling. Since he knew what had happened, I naturally thought he was speaking to me when, during one of his sermons, he said, "Tell your story."

"Tell my story?" I mumbled, cynically. "Who even wants to hear it?"

# 25

## THE LAST VISIT

*February 2007*
*Sarasota, Florida*

Altovise called to say she was in town for the weekend. She'd been traveling with Liza Minnelli, who was performing that week at Sarasota's Van Wezel Theater. She wanted to get together.

"Where are you staying?" I asked, expecting her to mention a hotel.

"With Tony and his wife," she responded.

"What?" I whispered in disbelief.

We made plans to get together the next day and she gave me directions to Tony's house.

The following afternoon, I found my way to the GreyHawk Landing community in Bradenton, and the winding road that led to Tony's street. I felt nervous as I reached for the doorbell. How would I be received?

Tony answered the door and looked startled for a moment. Then, he smiled and welcomed me in. Altovise was sitting under a hair dryer in the living room and she peeked out, looking perplexed as I entered. It dawned on me that I'd lost considerable weight and looked somewhat different from the last time she'd seen me.

"You look good," said Altovise, clearly surprised.

"You look good, too," I remarked, and reached over to hug her as she lifted up the dryer.

Tony's wife, Carol, was giving Altovise a new hairstyle, and while Altovise was getting ready, Tony gave me a tour of their home. The house was absolutely lovely and it was full of gorgeous paintings, many of which he'd painted. It took only a few moments to see that Tony had impeccable taste.

"And this is like one I gave to Frank Sinatra," he said, pointing to one that was presumably a copy.

Upstairs, there were magnificent antique furnishings, as well as evidence of Tony's considerable skills in carpentry. He devoted a great deal of time to cutting and assembling crafts in his garage, a workplace that was nothing less than his pride and joy. He told me that he'd screened it in, so he could work there throughout the year.

I had to admit, I was impressed.

That day, Altovise and I spent the bulk of the afternoon with her friend, Carl Mazu, and several of his friends who were visiting from his hometown in Pennsylvania. We talked at the bar at Marina Jack Restaurant for hours. It was a popular spot located right on the bay, and although it boasted a beautiful view, we didn't see much of it, not from the barstools.

Since I wasn't feeling well, I drank several glasses of cranberry juice. Altovise's drinks were considerably stronger, yet, she never slurred her words or exhibited any evidence of inebriation. At the end of the afternoon, she strutted out of the place with the same assured footing with which she'd entered. I was amazed.

During the long ride home, Altovised shared her thoughts about the day. She was especially concerned about Carl's health. In her opinion, he was just a wonderful man who was never ostentatious. "Never has to show off what he has," she noted. At that moment, I realized that she was actually thinking of someone else.

Altovise's travel plans were delayed the following day, when a storm in the Midwest caused the cancellation of her flight to L.A. Much to her dismay, she would miss all the exciting events surrounding the

Academy Awards, which were scheduled for that evening. While she wasn't planning to attend the actual ceremony, she was looking forward to hanging out at the after-Oscar parties. Now, unfortunately, she was stuck in Florida.

I knew that it was hard to be stranded on the other side of the country on Oscar night. Aside from New Year's Eve, this was probably the most glamorous evening of the year – at least, in Los Angeles. Regrettably, as we drove through the Sarasota-Bradenton area, it seemed like the quietest night of all.

Nonetheless, I invited Altovise to have dinner with Sandra and myself. Looking for signs of life, we opted to go to Chili's for dinner and found that a number of employees were actually watching the Oscars on a T.V. in the kitchen. Altovise told our waitress that she was supposed to be there for the events, and when the woman learned who she was, she quickly brought her manager over to meet her. Throughout the evening, she'd keep us updated on the progress of the show.

During dinner, Altovise got a call from a friend. The woman actually called twice, and during the last conversation, Altovise seemed pleased by something she'd said. Afterward, she told me that her friend was Paris Hilton's former dog sitter. They were planning to go shopping together just as soon as Altovise returned. They were specifically hunting for gowns that were worn to the Oscars. Her friend had already spotted one that she wanted.

"You know, they never wear them twice," Altovise said. "There's this place where you can buy them afterwards, and they're sold at a huge discount."

I must have had a blank expression, because I couldn't imagine what the final price might be, or where I'd even go in such an outfit.

Altovise looked surprised that I wasn't interested in buying one.

"I'd rather have one of your ruby slippers," I said.

Altovise looked puzzled.

"You know. One of the slippers from **The Wizard of Oz**," I said. "You still have them, don't you?"

"Oh, yes," she replied. "But, I've got some that are much prettier."

Now, I was confused. Did she think I was talking about wearing them?

"No," I said, clarifying my words. "Not to wear. Actually, I just want to hold them… see them. That was my favorite movie when I was growing up, and I always loved Judy Garland."

I knew that Liza Minnelli (Judy's daughter) had been very close to Sammy, and that she'd once given him the slippers as a special gift.

Half joking, I said, "If anything ever happens to you, Alto… leave me the slippers."

She nodded.

On the way back to Tony's house, Altovise was preoccupied and unusually quiet. I wasn't going to meddle, so I left her to her thoughts. But, as we turned into Tony's subdivision, she divulged something that was bothering her. She started by telling me about some research she was doing in New York, when she stumbled onto a document that gave someone the power of attorney over her affairs.

I acknowledged this and kept driving.

"But, it wasn't my signature on that document," she said.

The road was dark, and a shiver went through me.

"What are you saying?" I asked.

"Someone forged my signature," she replied, which essentially gave the person full control of her interest in Sammy's estate. Altovise went on to say that, if she was ever ill, they had the authority to determine whether or not she got life support.

"Alto," I stuttered, barely unable to speak. "What on earth is going on?" Struggling to find the right words, I delicately asked if it was possible that she'd signed the paper when she was in an "altered state of mind." After all, she could have been intoxicated. She may have simply forgotten that she'd signed it.

Altovise, however, was not only adamant that she hadn't signed it, but said she also recognized the handwriting.

"You have to do something!" I told her.

"I know," she said.

"You can't let that be the final document, the final word!" I stressed. "You've got to get a lawyer to write something that nullifies that... or supersedes it, or something!"

It was a pivotal moment, the first in which I'd insist that Altovise take action. From that night on, I'd continue to hound her about executing a new will, even if she had to do it online.

When I reached Tony's cul-de-sac, I turned onto the street and slowed in front of his house.

My heart felt like it was racing.

As Altovise gathered her things and opened the door, I asked, without thinking, the question that immediately came to me. "Alto, why do you stay with someone that you can't even trust?"

That moment would be firmly etched in my mind, because it would be the last time we'd be together.

Altovise glanced at me, smiling strangely as she got out of the car. Then, just before she closed the door, she paused and said, "Well, it's like Sammy always told me, 'Always keep your friends close to you... and your enemies even closer.'"

# 26

## A FILM'S HELD HOSTAGE

*2007-2009*
*Sarasota, Florida*

I contacted my literary agent, determined to finally write Altovise's story. It was the first time I'd felt a sense of urgency to publish it, but my agent didn't embrace the same views. She insisted that the only viable story was about the period in which Altovise spent with her husband. I knew, though, that the real message was the one which was in my heart. I needed to share the truth about what I'd witnessed and the nature of Altovise's ongoing struggles. The agent, however, felt that the only interested readers were those who wanted to know more about Sammy. She suggested that I write about their marriage. So, I attempted to begin the project, but my heart wasn't committed to it and I left it unfinished.

Oddly enough, Altovise and I grew closer in the following seasons, though our conversations were limited to the phone. We always planned to get together, but we always seemed to put it off. Still, our lives became more entwined, and this was mainly due to the extraordinary events that would take place.

Altovise, now, spent more time in California than New York. She moved from Barrett's townhouse after he offered her an apartment in a multi-family building that he'd acquired. She told me that his office was located in a unit somewhere above hers. She wasn't terribly happy with the arrangement, but, at least, when she was on the West Coast, she had her own space.

I, too, was uncomfortable with this situation, but felt relieved knowing that Altovise had a close friend looking after her. She often spoke about Tina Allen, the famed sculptor who was commissioned to create Sammy's statue. I'd never met Tina, but from what I'd heard, she sounded like she was as solid as a rock and the type of dependable friend whom Altovise could trust. It seemed like her integrity was expressed in the quality of her work. One of the artist's most famous projects was her thirteen-foot bronze statue of **Roots** author, Alex Haley. One of her most recent works – that of abolitionist, Frederick Douglass – was featured in the highly acclaimed film, **Akeela and the Bee.**

"Did you see that movie?" asked Altovise. "That was Tina's work!"

Increasingly, Tina's name came up in our conversations. She was often present when Altovise called me. During one of our talks, she mentioned that Tina had a disagreement with Barrett because he hadn't paid her for the work on Sammy's statue. Altovise also complained at length about problems she'd had with Barrett, and said she believed that he'd gone through her dresser drawers.

"My favorite ring and bracelet set that Sammy gave me are gone," she said. "Burt Boyar told me not to worry too much over it. They'd have another set made, just like the original one."

Altovise, however, didn't want another set, because it wouldn't replace the sentimental value attached to the one that Sammy gave her.

In a later conversation, Altovise advised me that she'd moved to a new place on West Olympic Boulevard. She said that Barrett became incensed when she refused to sign another form that he'd brought and during their argument, he'd kicked her out of the apartment. She said that she was actually relieved to be away from him and reminded me that he'd gone through her personal things. Regrettably, Altovise hadn't had enough time to pack up all her things.

"Forget those things," I said. "Just be glad you're out of there."

"You're right," she said.

I warned her to stay away from Barrett.

"But I do miss the children," she lamented.

"I'm not kidding," I said. "Keep a safe distance from him."

In January 2008, Altovise filed a lawsuit against Barrett LaRoda and Anthony Francis for "allegedly tricking her into signing away" her intellectual property rights to Sammy's work for a third of the shares of the company they formed. In the documents were complaints that her former partners exaggerated their show business credentials, defrauded her, and brought negotiations for the movie based on Sammy's life to a halt when they demanded fees and executive producer credits without consulting her. Joining the suit was Burt Boyar and his company, Boyar Investments LLC of Dallas, Texas.

Frankly, I was stunned when Altovise finally took a stand, but I was proud of her for finding the courage to speak up. The case was filed in Dallas, Texas. After she asked me to write down the events that I'd witnessed for her attorney, I faxed the deposition to the Dallas hotel where she was then staying. One or two days later, the parties gathered in two separate rooms in a mediator's office, not far from the courthouse. No settlement was reached. In fact, it was only the beginning of a case which only grew more complicated.

"Barrett came with three lawyers," said Altovise, still amazed. "I wonder how much he's paying them."

On April 8, Altovise called around 11:00 p.m. She needed to talk. She'd hoped that they'd reach a settlement, but they'd failed to come to an agreement. Barrett wanted approximately $500,000 to let her out of their contract. Altovise, however, saw a light at the end of her tunnel and she began to think more clearly. She realized that their partnership agreement expired in May 2009. If Barrett could hold the movie hostage by holding out for upfront fees, she could hold out, herself, until their contract expired. In fact, as the months passed, Altovise became more adamant about this, and held on to this strategy. She decided that her former partners wouldn't get another cent from her.

"They've taken me to the cleaners!" she declared.

In another conversation, Altovise spoke of an incident which had occurred during the movie negotiations. Barrett, she said, was supposed to have a meeting with Burt Boyar and Howard Bloomingdale, whom she hoped would be one of the film's producers. Barrett was scheduled to meet with the two men at a restaurant, but arrived an hour and a half late. Then, she was told, he started yelling and screaming at them. She said, after that, he "took off in his car like a crazy man."

Barrett later yelled at Altovise: "Why should they be producers? I want my money up front!"

Altovise, thoroughly frustrated, said, "This thing is holding up the movie, because they don't want any part of LaRoda. He's unprofessional and inexperienced."

As expected, Barrett and Tony launched a countersuit against Altovise, Burt Boyar and the others who were connected to the film. During this time the case was moved to Los Angeles.

Each season seemed to be filled with problems, so I waited before telling Altovise about the package I'd received from Art Rutter. Inside the box were all four copies of our screenplay, as well as the original material, enclosed with a note. The brief message didn't explain what had happened or why he still had the copies. It only indicated that he'd moved to another agency, Innovative Artists, in Santa Monica.

# 27

## THE KING'S LAST PARTY

*Early September 2008*
*Sarasota, Florida*

Altovise went to Michael Jackson's birthday party. She didn't mention that it was his fiftieth, and, of course, had no way of knowing that it would be his last. She did mention that the phenomenal entertainer was inspired by Sammy, and had always looked up to him as a mentor. In fact, she said that Michael performed in a special tribute to Sammy.

"Really?" I replied, thinking I'd locate the performance on YouTube.

"Oh, yes," said Altovise, before going back to her memories of the party.

"I was sitting at Michael's table," she said. "And I saw Londell McMillan come over and try to talk with him."

Altovise didn't seem to know that McMillan represented the Jackson's family.

"Anyway, Londell said that he wanted to talk with me," she continued. "But, I never did speak with him."

"He's not your attorney anymore, is he?" I asked.

"No," she replied.

# 28

## A SEASON OF MOURNING BEGINS

*Week of September 9, 2008*
*Sarasota, Florida*

For about a week, I tried to reach Altovise, but was unsuccessful. I wondered if she was having the same type of trouble with her phone as she had with her Internet service. I kept trying, but got no answer.

After four or five days, I became very worried. It dawned on me that I didn't have phone numbers for any of Altovise's neighbors. She'd once given me a friend's number, but I'd misplaced it. I wanted to kick myself, because I'd meant to get Tina's number, in case of an emergency. So, I decided to look up her Web site and phone number on the Internet. First, however, I'd try once more to reach Altovise.

To my amazement, she finally answered the phone. However, she sounded ill. Her voice was very faint.

"Are you okay?" I asked.

It took her a moment to get her words out, but when she spoke, I nearly dropped the phone.

"Tina died," she said, clearly shocked.

"What?" I shrieked. "I was just about to call her! I've been trying to find you! What happened? Was she sick?"

Altovise was trying to say something, but I couldn't make it out.

"Wasn't she young? What on earth happened?"

Altovise said she'd had a heart attack.

"Are you okay?" I asked. "Where are you?"

"In Las Vegas," she said. "But, I'm heading home now."

Once assured that she was safe and traveling with friends, I told her to call as soon as she got there.

Afterwards, I sat on my bed, totally stunned. The famous sculptor, Tina Allen, had passed away and she was only fifty-eight.

# 29

## A FLOWER BLOOMS IN THE DESERT

*October 2008*
*Sarasota, Florida*

Altovise was shaken by Tina's death and would often speak about the arrangements for her memorial service. Tina's daughter was expecting a child and couldn't travel from Georgia until November, so the service was delayed. This subject came up in nearly every conversation, as it seemed to dominate Altovise's thoughts. I was worried, because she wasn't adjusting very well to the loss of her friend.

In the meantime, I'd also had some adjustments to make. I'd had my tenth hip surgery and it had knocked me off my feet for several months. My recovery was slower than expected and I was still walking with a cane. Several personal problems had magnified the glumness of the season, so I could certainly relate to Altovise's feeling of sadness.

During one of our conversations, I shared something that I thought would be uplifting. It was a new project I'd started at a charter school. Earlier, I'd begun to offer video production services, creating a few documentaries about a friend's motivational program for students. The mission of its founder was to incentivize and reward students for high scholastic achievement. I wanted to devote more time to this initiative, but didn't know the best way to pursue it.

That fall, however, I was given a brief opportunity to do something very creative. I offered a 'writing-to-video' contest at the school. Once the winning story was selected, several middle school students would use it to produce their own video. The entries we received were amazing, and we finally narrowed the selection down to one winning narrative: the true story of a girl who'd conquered a life-threatening disease.

I told Altovise about the story. As a baby, the girl had suffered from a rare condition which became so severe she was hospitalized for a couple of years. When the doctors gave up on her, they removed all of her tubes and said she only had weeks to live. She prayed, however, and by faith, believed that she'd recovered. The following day she asked her physicians to take one more test, and to their amazement, she was perfectly well. Her faith had healed her and it was a miracle story that everyone loved.

Altovise was touched by the story. She wanted more details about the project. It was inspiring for many reasons. The beauty of the story was, it had the potential to actually transform the lives of other children. Kids who'd never held cameras, performed as actors, or edited videos, would produce a powerful full-length video about their classmate. In bringing her story to the screen, they were empowered to do something they'd never thought possible. Already, one could see the transformation taking place, as they grew more confident each day and it was wonderful.

We both seemed to experience a twinge of excitement, and as we talked about the video, we considered doing the same thing with our story. Maybe it was time to finally bring *A Detour to Mexico* to life.

During the following weeks, Altovise and I talked about this idea and explored several options. We wanted to do something innovative for kids, and stop just talking about it. Life was too short to just have dreams, but never achieve them, so we decided to start our own production company. Despite the setbacks we'd endured, we'd move forward with our stories. We'd form our own publishing division to create fun and motivational materials. We wanted to inspire kids to read more books and excel academically, just as Sammy had desired.

We'd use *A Detour to Mexico* to launch a national video contest and reward students who produced a powerful scene from the story. We'd also showcase the talent of gifted young artists, kids who wanted to sing, dance, act, or develop other types of artistry. In the process, we'd encourage them to read and write. We wanted to help kids appreciate the fact that all great movies came from great stories. It was a wonderful way to demonstrate that education and entertainment truly complemented each other.

Altovise and I were so thrilled by the idea that we could barely stop talking about it. I shared with her the motto I'd adopted: "It's cool to be smart!" She liked it, and chuckled as she repeated it.

"That's great!" she said. "That's perfect!"

We had no money and we weren't sure of what we were doing, but we were rich in terms of wonderful stories. We couldn't wait to finally share them with the world and decided to explore all opportunities to do so. Naturally, we turned to the Internet.

"We've got to get a team together," I said. "We can't do it alone." So, I started looking for partners and sponsors, and we called our company Lil' SamHat Productions.

Altovise wanted me to contact two brothers she knew. She said they'd expressed interest in helping out when she told them she wanted to write books and do something positive for kids. She said their names were Brian and Mark Cuban, and they were "very nice." I sent an e-mail to Brian, advising him that Altovise was trying to reach him. When he replied, he assured me that he'd call her. Altovise later gave me his phone number and suggested that I contact him directly. I preferred to send a detailed letter, via e-mail, and wait for a response.

Our minds were made up. We'd continue the work that we started, and just as Sammy asked, urge kids to get serious about their education. We would develop fun and inventive ways to support them, showcase their talent, and reward their academic achievements. What could be more exciting than this?

# 30

## DISAPPEARING ACTS

*Winter 2008*
*Sarasota, Florida*

ltovise called me one night, upset about money that was missing from her bank accounts. Then, approximately twenty minutes later, she called again to tell me that a friend had looked into various matters for her, and found that all her stock was gone. It amounted to some $20,000 worth of Israeli stocks which Sammy had acquired while visiting Israel many years before. I asked how this could have happened, and she said that Barrett had gained access by using his name as executor of the estate.

"But, Alto, didn't you advise all the banks and everyone that they're to honor only your signature?" I asked.

Although Altovise stuttered a bit, she said that she thought that she did.

In another conversation, Altovise told me that the royalty payments she routinely received had also stopped coming.

"Didn't you contact the companies to ensure that it was your name and address that they sent the checks to?" I asked.

"Yes," she said. "But, I don't know why they've stopped coming. I told them that the payments weren't to go to my former partners, but to me."

She was dumbfounded.

I was just as dumbstruck by another occurrence. A recent biography about Sammy seemed to focus an enormous amount of attention on Altovise's life. It casted such a negative impression of her, that it posed a real challenge to our newly formed company. In fact, a few people who'd expressed interest in working with us, immediately pulled out.

Altovise was shaken by a number of things that were written about her, but she decided to try to rise above it. Some of the material seemed to be based on speculation, and unfortunately, the author relied on information he'd obtained from some of Altovise's main adversaries. As incredible as it seemed, Barrett and Tony were interviewed and their views were included in the book, but the author never sat down to talk with Altovise. This was strange, since he'd written about very personal aspects of her life.

"He doesn't even know me," Altovise sighed. She couldn't understand why the book was written that way.

I, too, was perplexed, especially with regard to the last segment. The author wrote that Altovise had lived in California during a period in which she'd actually lived in Sarasota. That year, in fact, was 2005, the period in which I'd met her. What was most striking, or disturbing, was that if anyone simply accepted the author's version of what transpired, they'd never know something important about Altovise.

As I looked more closely, I began to wonder why there were deviations from what actually took place, even surrounding the circumstances that led Altovise to Sarasota. According to the book, she'd been in a rehabilitation facility in California and, against the advice of others, had recklessly resettled in California after leaving the facility. However, I'd heard from three sources (including Altovise) that she'd been in a program in Oklahoma – Narconon International – where she met Tracey. When the two women left, they moved to Sarasota, not to Los Angeles. After settling in the area that fall, Altovise's phone number was actually listed in the Sarasota directory.

Why did the author write that Altovise was in California all that time? That question frightened me. It was as though the events I'd experienced during the previous four years had never happened. The incidents that occurred had affected my life as dramatically as they'd affected Altovise's. Our only mistake was that we'd been silent about them.

"Altovise, you've got to speak up," I said. "I'm working on the book, and if you need it, you can use it. But, it's time you spoke up!"

Altovise was trying to restart her life, but she was being pulled down from every direction. It was unfair that she was denied an opportunity to address her own issues. She was working to establish a new career and was deeply devoted to helping young people. Extremely creative, she possessed a unique streak of brilliance, and loved to write children's stories. However, there was nothing written about her that indicated this, only images that portrayed her as an irresponsible alcoholic.

I believed that when people had a chance to get to know her – the real Altovise Davis – they would judge for themselves who she really was. I stressed this when we talked.

"Let your work speak for itself," I said. "When you reach out to make a difference, especially for children, people will know where your heart is."

I assured Altovise that I'd speed up the work. I'd try to complete the book, as well as get the company off the ground. Then, people would have a chance to see a broader picture of who she was. I felt guilty, however, and apologized for my slow pace.

Although, I'd had reconstructive surgery on my hip replacement – my tenth hip operation – the delay wasn't entirely due to my health issues, but to efforts to look after my other 'partner,' who was also battling with alcoholism. After losing his job, Grover, my fiancé suffered from a deep depression and couldn't seem to stop drinking. His life went into a complete tailspin. If I'd thought it would be easy to save his soul, I'd been naïve. Balancing the emotional trauma and the physical demands required to keep him safe (from himself), was like handling twenty-four-hour shifts of crisis intervention. I was frazzled.

"Hang in there," I told her. "I'm working as fast as I can."

Altovise called a few times, needing help in another area. A contact in the Bahamas had alerted her that someone was trying to sell the three undeveloped lots she owned there. Sammy had given them to her around the time they were married. She told the realtors not to deal with anyone but her. Then, she began to wonder if, perhaps, she should sell the property. Ironically, there was a purchaser wanting to make an offer.

"Should I sell them?" she asked.

"Let me check on something first," I replied.

Having been a former realtor, I wanted to do some research. I contacted two real estate agents in the area, and asked each one for a comparable market analysis. Their figures confirmed what I suspected. The offer was much too low.

"Don't take it," I said, when I called back. "Keep them and develop them yourself."

Then, I said, "I'll pray about all this."

The stressful nature of my New Year's Eve celebration led to reflections on the previous twelve months, and I felt depressed. Still, I knew that things could have been worse, and there were blessings for which I should have been thankful. After all, I'd actually found a wonderful surgeon in the area; otherwise I would have had to travel to another state for my surgery.

Dr. Edward Stolarski was the only specialist in town who was considered qualified to operate on my hip, as he handled complicated revisions of hip replacements. After viewing my X-rays, he quickly made arrangements to include me in his heavy schedule, because my right hip needed urgent attention. He later commented that he didn't know how I'd been able to walk with my hip in its condition. The joint was on the verse of collapsing. Like my other doctors, he seemed to wonder what on earth I'd been doing. Truth be told, I'd been fairly busy, but since I didn't have much to show for it, I just smiled and thanked him for saving my hip.

My hip may have been saved, but nearly everything else in my life began to collapse.

# 31

## END OF THE CHAPTER

*January 2009*
*Sarasota, Florida*

Altovise was stressed out by a multitude of new pressures, as various parties directly, or indirectly, urged her to pay off her former partners. She said that, Burt, in particular, wanted to move forward with the movie deal, stressing that he wasn't young anymore and wanted to see the film done while he was still around. By now, however, it had gotten very personal, at least, as far as Altovise was concerned. She said that Barrett first demanded $500,000 to walk away, but when they tried to meet his offer, he'd upped the ante to a million. Altovise felt strongly opposed to giving him this. She felt he'd already taken too much from her and she wasn't going to budge.

"Besides," she said confidently, "within only a few months, our contract expires." She'd stuck it out this long and she felt it was worth it. That date in May was now close at hand.

Still, all the pressures and disappointments were beginning to take a toll. Altovise was also still grieving over Tina's death. Then, she mentioned a cousin she'd visited at a hospital and he, too, had passed away. Each time we spoke, she brought this up as though it were the first time she'd mentioned it.

"There's no one you can really trust," Altovise said one night. She felt alone because she didn't have any relatives out there. I felt badly for Altovise and wished that she'd stayed in Sarasota. There were too many pressures on her and there was no one she could depend on. I knew she felt hurt over the things written about her in the book, as she was now getting quite a bit of feedback from various acquaintances.

"That guy didn't even know me," she said, again.

Once more, she complained about the missing jewelry and money taken from her accounts, and she was still upset about the checks that had stopped coming in.

I was also concerned about her finances and asked, "Alto, didn't you get paid for that book project you did with Burt?"

"That's what I'm talkin' about," said Altovise. "That's what I thought, but…"

I recalled that when she left Sarasota to handle some business deals in L.A., the photo book was near the top of her priorities. Since then, the book had been published, but there was an unanswered question.

"Alto, didn't you sign the contract for that book?" I asked.

"Well… I think…" she stammered.

I'd seen the book in the bookstore, and although Altovise provided numerous pictures, I'd only spotted a note of acknowledgment thanking her for the contribution. I didn't see her listed as a co-author.

In that latest biography, inferences were also made about this omission. Tracey Davis, Altovise's step-daughter, apparently felt cheated and verbalized her belief (or suspicion) that Altovise would have been paid for the photo book. I wondered, however, why it appeared that she wasn't. Burt Boyar, with rather peculiar wording, seemed to imply that he didn't want to get Altovise into any tax trouble. I wondered about this, too. How could she get into trouble if she wasn't a co-author and didn't receive any of the proceeds? Or did she? Like everything else, this was very mysterious.

"Do you remember meeting with an agent, or publisher," I asked, ". . . to discuss an advance or any other payments?"

"I've got to look into that," Altovise replied, obviously confused.

I didn't have the heart to tell her that, if she hadn't signed the contract, it was much too late. It was a done deal. Although I was curious, I couldn't bring myself to ask about the number of pictures she'd provided. Did she contribute forty percent, sixty, or even ninety percent of the book's material?

My head was now flooded with questions. I wondered what the trip to L.A. had actually accomplished.

In the weeks that followed, Altovise called on two occasions to share good news. The first time, she phoned right after leaving her attorney's office. She was so excited that she hadn't even waited until she got home. She said that my assistance had been helpful and she felt optimistic about gaining a favorable outcome in her case.

Then, when she called the second time, she mentioned that she'd been exonerated from the debt she still owned. I was so excited that I neglected to ask if the news came from her attorney or an accountant.

"That's wonderful!" I shrieked. "Is that just on the federal level or is it also the State of California?"

"Well, I'm not completely sure," she replied, since she'd just heard the news. "I'll call and find out the details."

Our next conversation was sobered by the fact that we both had the flu. She had called me that night, but I was so congested that I told her I'd have to call her back.

About a week later, at my friend's school, a fourth grade teacher left and I was asked to help out with her class. It was an opportunity to actually make a real difference with real kids, he stressed. The opportunity was exciting, but my insecurities about my health made me nervous. Did I really have the strength and stamina needed to keep up with a room full of youngsters? If I was able to hold down a full-time position, I could overcome some of my financial problems, and devote significant resources toward our business. Maybe, it was time to take a chance. I prayed that I was healthy enough to do this.

# 32

## THE LAST PAGE

*March 16, 2009*
*Sarasota, Florida*

The phone rang around 1:30 in the morning. Assuming that I was asleep, my mother quickly answered it and decided against awakening me. She waited until about 7:00 a.m. to talk with me.

I was making a salad for lunch when she called me to her bedroom. Still carrying a bag of fresh spinach, I opened her door to see if she was alright. She started to speak, but I couldn't understand what she was saying.

"A man called late last night," she began. "But, I didn't want to awaken you."

"Yes," I replied. "I heard the phone ring. I wasn't really asleep."

She was looking down at a piece of paper, telling me that Manny had called.

"Who?" I asked, because I barely heard her.

"Manny," she repeated. "He said his mother died."

"What?" I said, not understanding. "His mother? Who?"

Clearing her throat, she said, "Altovise died."

"What?" I screamed, dropping the bag. "No, that can't be! No!"

She repeated the news as my father silently looked up at me, "Altovise had a stroke and she died. Manny left his number."

I ran to my room, and dropped to my knees to pray, "God, no! Please, not like this. Please, let it be a mistake!"

I was so shocked, I could barely speak.

# 33

## THE WILL AND ESTATE

*Following Seasons*
*Sarasota, Florida*

I was deeply saddened by Altovise's death. During our first conversation, I told Manny of my close friendship with his mother and how much she'd loved him. I mentioned that, when we'd created our screenplay, Altovise had thought of him when she envisioned one of our main characters. Then, I informed him that his mother had executed a new will so that his inheritance would be protected, and urged him to find the document as soon as possible.

I'd encouraged Altovise to use an online legal service, particularly the one I'd researched when I was preparing the contract to form our company. It was called LegalZoom.com, and it seemed ideal for her, since she needed a quick and affordable new will.

Altovise, however, was leery of the company, but I assured her that, if Robert Shapiro was its founder, then it had to be a legitimate legal firm. After all, he was a famous attorney from the O.J. Simpson case. After giving it some thought, Altovise finally agreed, and I emailed to her the link to their website.

That spring, I was so grief-stricken that I couldn't fully appreciate the importance of these actions. This was especially true, a month and a half later, when another shocking tragedy would occur.

I'd just enrolled Grover, my fiancé, in a faith-based alcohol re-hab program. Although, he'd been unhappy with my choice – and complained about the long, nearly two hour distance between us – I felt that the program's peaceful and rural farm setting was the ideal place for him to detox and heal.

Grover desperately needed help. Unable to find employment af-ter losing his job, he'd started drinking uncontrollably. I'd never seen him so unstable and I was terrified for his safety. Grover, however, was leery about entering the program, because it had a reputation for being one of the toughest, which – among other things – meant he wouldn't be allowed any visitors, or the use of a cell phone, for the first thirty days. We'd never been separated by such a long distance, so it was hard on both of us.

Altovise died on March 14th, during the first week in which Grover was finally allowed to have guests. Although, I was sched-uled to visit him, I was still reeling from the shock of her death and cancelled my trip. I called the facility and left a message for Grover with one of the directors, but no one gave it to him until four days later.

During the following days, Grover started to panic. Already de-pressed, he became further disheartened. He had desperately want-ed to change and redeem his life, but he was rapidly losing faith that he'd succeed. Instead, he dwelled on all the mistakes he'd made and the painful consequences he'd had to suffer.

Grover had worried incessantly about his age, his troubled past, and the impact of the recession on his employability. And then, there was the prospect of our wedding, which had been postponed for over a year. Would it really happen?

No one at the program seemed to have been watching Grover closely enough to notice that he was losing hope and giving up. When I didn't arrive, he mistakenly believed that I, too, had given up on him.

Thirty-five days after Altovise's death, Grover died from a massive seizure and heart attack after drinking a lethal dose of antifreeze. I'd spent the last three days at his bedside in a hospital as he laid there in a coma, and I was in shock.

Grover's death was so devastating that I couldn't get through the following months without crying. Each day, I held my stomach as I continually battled with nausea. I couldn't utter the word 'suicide' for over a year, nor reread the last letters which he'd sent me.

Losing both of my partners so tragically, left a gaping hole in my heart. I felt an enormous sense of guilt, and continually asked, "Why?"

"Why hadn't I seen it coming? Why had I urged them to stand strong? Why had I given them a false sense of hope?"

Desperate for answers, I began to research and produce inspirational documentaries, particularly for people who were going through the mourning process and other painful losses in their lives. Within the following two years, I'd hire Geoffrey Owens to host a web show that I called, *The Witness to Miracles and Angels.* The show was specifically about heaven and the afterlife experience. I felt that Geoffrey was a gifted, Shakespearean-trained actor who would offer a rich and professional quality to the documentary. Wanting the very best, I also hired an Emmy-award winning editor and cameraman.

The project also offered an opportunity to support Geoffrey's work. A friend had confided in me that, she'd personally drawn up the contracts for *The Cosby Show*, applying the standard pay scale that was used for all actors appearing in T.V. sitcoms. Bill Cosby, however, had sent the contracts back, demanding that the salary of his co-stars be cut, so that his would be increased. Knowing this, I understood why Geoffrey was sometimes very short on cash, but I never brought it up.

For me, it was a special ministry project, and it included the production of mini-documentaries and testimonies of people who'd overcome substance abuse. The projects would actually help me get through the hardest years of my life.

It was difficult to sit down and chronicle the terrible events that preceded Altovise's death, but she'd been very upset about the scandalous passages written about her, and I felt obligated to speak up on her behalf. I recorded the incidents I'd witnessed in a self-published book entitled, ***The Last Chapter in the Life of Mrs. Sammy Davis Jr.***

Manny Davis and his attorney, Olu Orange, would later read my book and contact me to express their appreciation. The steps that I'd taken, and the events that I'd recorded, played a vital role in the court's later decision that Manny was the rightful heir to the Sammy Davis Jr. Estate.

After the legal and financial encumbrances were eventually cleared, the estate would be valued at approximately $10 million. Although, the validity of Altovise's final will was contested – the LegalZoom document that I'd insisted she use – a California judge would also uphold its legitimacy.

Years later, when I looked back on these events, they would represent the most painful years of my life. Admittedly, my faith had been severely tested, but the miracles that I witnessed and documented for others, would eventually heal my own heart and strengthen my faith.

Although, I still battled with the guilt of having lost, both, Altovise and Grover, there was one indisputable fact that offered some degree of comfort. Despite all the things that had gone wrong, I'd actually saved the Sammy Davis Jr. Estate.

# EPILOGUE

In the summer of 2015, ten years after Altovise and I created the screenplay, *A Detour to Mexico,* I made plans to continue our work by producing the film. True to our vision, I started the groundwork needed to launch various competitions to showcase the talent of undiscovered stars. In many ways, the film project would represent a 'life-imitating-art' scenario, as the main characters in *A Detour to Mexico* were, themselves, competing in an international talent contest. Their journey, like our own, was delayed by unexpected and difficult challenges.

Admittedly, I faced some apprehension about moving forward with the film. However, just as I was about to back out, I heard a timely message from Pastor T.D. Jakes. In a touching sermon from a radio broadcast, he basically said that, if one didn't finish what they'd committed themselves to do, they'd never feel good about themselves. We had to persevere through the tough times to experience the blessing on the other side.

I smiled when I heard his words, knowing that I'd turned on the car radio at just the right time. The pastor's message conveyed the same essential theme we'd tried to deliver in our story.

With RisingStar31, my production company, I returned to my original mission: to inspire and encourage people – both, young and old – to hold fast to their dreams, no matter what challenges they faced. From my own experiences, I'd gained a great appreciation for the motto which I now share with others: *God is love, so whatever you do, and whatever you create, do it with love. Love never fails.*

# SELECTED BIBLIOGRAPHY

Birkbeck, Matt. *Deconstructing Sammy*. New York: HarperCollins, 2008.

Davis, Sammy, Jr., and Jane and Burt Boyar. *Why Me? The Sammy Davis Jr. Story*. New York: Farrar, Straus and Giroux, 1989.

Fishgall, Gary. *Gonna Do Great Things: The Life of Sammy Davis Jr.* New York: Scribner, 2003.

Haygood, Wil. *In Black and White*. New York: Billboard Books, 2003.

Poitier, Sidney. *This Life.* New York: Knopf, 1980.

**Pamela Sherrod** is an author, screenwriter, speaker and documentary producer. She graduated from Howard University with a B.A. in Journalism. That year, she served as a Congressional Intern, where she attended congressional hearings, conducted research and helped prepare legislative briefings. In the following year, she scheduled group tours of the White House, Capitol, and FBI Building.

Pamela later took a position at the ABC News Washington Bureau. As a news assistant, she helped produce *Nightline, World News Tonight with Peter Jennings, This Week with David Brinkley* **and** *Sunday World News with Carole Simpson (and Sam Donaldson).*

During the following years, she held various positions and was the coordinator of a Crisis Intervention program for women in Connecticut, a role which inspired her to become an advocate for women and girls.

Among other books, Pamela is the author of the biography, *The Last Chapter in the Life of Mrs. Sammy Davis, Jr.* Her articles have appeared in *Black Enterprise* and other publications.

As a screenwriter, Pamela partnered with the late Altovise Davis, and formed a production company to write and produce entertaining and educational films. The first screenplay that they coauthored was *A Detour to Mexico.*

Pamela is the founder of RisingStar31 Productions, a team which consists of professional videographers, on air talent, and a postproduction crew which includes an Emmy Award winning editor. Her projects include inspirational documentaries, book trailers and other promotional videos. Pamela produced the web show called, *The Witness to Miracles and Angels,* which was hosted by actor, Geoffrey Owens.

In 2015, Pamela launched plans to produce her first musical film, *A Detour to Mexico.*

She currently lives in Sarasota, Florida, where she's raising her daughter.